Praise for *Deliberate Exc[...]*

Dynamic leadership matters! Dr. Dance's remarkable journey [...] inspired him to develop a blueprint for educational leadership excellence. Fighting for equitable practices and outcomes for all children is clearly his passion. Every administrator or aspiring leader will flourish if these principles are put into action!

—Cheryl R. Brooks, Principal
Berkshire Elementary School
Baltimore, MD

I wish I had read *Deliberate Excellence* 20 years ago! Providing a road map for leaders wishing to affect significant change, Dallas Dance's book balances theory with practical experiences. Dr. Dance outlines his bold and successful tactics to address the complex equity issues that plague school districts. His strategic approach to communications is a model for all school administrators.

—Luvelle Brown, Superintendent
Ithaca City School District
Ithaca, NY

For 20 years, Dr. Dallas Dance has been an inspiration to me as a leader. He understands that true leaders inspire others to lead, galvanize their audience, and provide practical applications to difficult situations. Regardless of the political climate, Dr. Dance has always kept students first. After reading *Deliberate Excellence*, educators will take away successful strategies to increase student achievement.

—John B. Gordon III, Chief of Schools
Chesterfield County Public Schools
Chesterfield, VA

Deliberate Excellence is a book written for all leaders. Dr. Dallas Dance speaks from real-life experiences that are relatable and from the heart. His leadership steps have helped him develop into one of the most accomplished administrative leaders in the country. The three specific strategies outlined in this book will transform your leadership skills and help you stay on track to ensure success.

—Susan Monaghan, Principal
Westbury High School
Houston, TX

As an educational leader with 30 years' experience, I've read many books on leadership. Dr. Dance's book is a must-read for all educators. By sharing real stories, he keeps the focus on equity, change management, and communication. *Deliberate Excellence* is an insightful read from the heart of a leader on the fundamental strategies that should drive educational leaders.

—Martha Salazar-Zamora,
Superintendent of Schools
Tomball Independent School District
Tomball, TX

In education today, the question is not whether or not we must embrace and lead for change—the question is how we do that in a way that changes lives and secures a real future for our students. In *Deliberate Excellence*, we are given a resource that answers this question for every leader seeking to understand what it takes to move his or her district forward. Dr. Dance makes an inspiring case for why we should be doing this work and the important role our leadership has to play in the lives of our children and our communities. Fortunately for us, he draws on his experiences as a model leader to create a guidebook filled with compelling anecdotes and positive advice that can be used right away.

—**Aaron C. Spence, Superintendent**
Virginia Beach City Public Schools
Virginia Beach, VA

Deliberate Excellence shows educational leaders how to increase agency within their organizations. This book effectively communicates the importance of engaging in challenging work to improve schools and districts, which is what the head, hand, and heart of education is all about. I applaud Dr. Dance for his extraordinary leadership during unordinary times.

—**Andre D. Spencer, Superintendent**
Harrison School District Two
Colorado Springs, CO

Dr. Dance has demonstrated the power of enlightened leadership to transform schools. As one of the most accomplished leaders I've seen, he understands how to work with all parties to accomplish what only a handful of school systems can claim: substantially improved educational outcomes for children from all racial and ethnic groups.

—**Freeman Hrabowski, President**
University of Maryland Baltimore County

What Dallas has done as a bold and innovative educational leader is nothing short of amazing. What I saw under his leadership was a school system that wasn't afraid to tackle big complex issues, particularly around equity, and get results.

—**Arne Duncan,**
Former U.S. Secretary of Education

Deliberate Excellence

*This book is dedicated to my late grandmother,
Hydelia Cotman, who would stop at nothing to ensure that in
working with my mother, my life would be the richest it could possibly
be. You sacrificed so much to keep our family going. And you continue
to watch over us as our biggest angel. I love and miss you dearly.*

*And to the many educators who wake up each day committed
to providing equitable opportunities for all students and who are
committed to growing and getting better each day. Let us continue to
motivate and support each other as we continue leading the work.*

Deliberate Excellence

Three Fundamental Strategies That Drive Educational Leadership

S. Dallas Dance

Foreword by Rod Paige

CORWIN
A SAGE Publishing Company

A SAGE Publishing Company

FOR INFORMATION:

Corwin
A SAGE Company
2455 Teller Road
Thousand Oaks, California 91320
(800) 233-9936
www.corwin.com

SAGE Publications Ltd.
1 Oliver's Yard
55 City Road
London EC1Y 1SP
United Kingdom

SAGE Publications India Pvt. Ltd.
B 1/I 1 Mohan Cooperative Industrial Area
Mathura Road, New Delhi 110 044
India

SAGE Publications Asia-Pacific Pte. Ltd.
3 Church Street
#10-04 Samsung Hub
Singapore 049483

Printed in the United States of America

Library of Congress Cataloging-in-Publication Data

Names: Dance, S. Dallas, author.

Title: Deliberate excellence : three fundamental strategies that drive educational leadership / S. Dallas Dance.

Description: Thousand Oaks, California : Corwin, a SAGE Company, 2018. | Includes bibliographical references and index.

Identifiers: LCCN 2017034662 | ISBN 9781506392011 (pbk. : acid-free paper)

Subjects: LCSH: Dance, S. Dallas. | School superintendents—Maryland—Baltimore County—Biography. | Educational leadership—Maryland—Baltimore County. | Educational change—Maryland—Baltimore County. | Baltimore County Public Schools—Administration.

Classification: LCC LB2831.724.M37 D36 2018 | DDC 371.2—dc23
LC record available at https://lccn.loc.gov/2017034662

This book is printed on acid-free paper.

Publisher: Arnis Burvikovs
Development Editor: Desirée A. Bartlett
Editorial Assistants: Kaitlyn Irwin and
                                 Eliza Riegert
Production Editor: Amy Schroller
Copy Editor: Megan Markanich
Typesetter: C&M Digitals (P) Ltd.
Proofreader: Dennis W. Webb
Indexer: Amy Murphy
Cover Designer: Rose Storey
Marketing Manager: Nicole Franks

Certified Chain of Custody
SUSTAINABLE FORESTRY INITIATIVE
Promoting Sustainable Forestry
www.sfiprogram.org
SFI-01268

SFI label applies to text stock

17 18 19 20 21 10 9 8 7 6 5 4 3 2 1

CONTENTS

Please view the link at this QR code to read a message from S. Dallas Dance that discusses his current plans and ongoing work.

FOREWORD

Rod Paige

As the former U.S. secretary of education and superintendent of the nation's seventh largest school district, I know firsthand the heavy leadership lift that must occur for transformational change to happen and, most importantly, to be sustainable. Heart, passion, and an unyielding belief in kids and the work must be the foundation. Very few educational leaders actually accomplish this task, especially in large, diverse school systems.

Equity was the hallmark of Dr. Dance's tenure as superintendent of Baltimore County Public Schools (BCPS), which encompasses rural, suburban, and urban neighborhoods. Its demographics shifted dramatically during the past thirty years. Now, 60 percent are students of color, and 45 percent are eligible for free or reduced-price meals. Among an increasing enrollment of more than 112,000, the fastest growing groups of students are those demonstrating significant needs: students receiving special education services and English language learners.

Change is hard. However, under Dr. Dance's leadership, a large, diverse school system showed student progress.

- Elementary students made impressive gains on the nationally normed Measures of Academic Progress, which sets individual student growth targets toward college and career readiness.

- The graduation rate gap between black and white students closed in 2015.

- And graduation rates continue to increase for students of every race and ethnicity to nearly 90 percent at the end of his tenure.

Four Elements of Success

Four elements for success emerged from Blueprint 2.0, a strategic plan focused on equity, or meeting individual student needs.

First, *equity* was defined and discussed as the central goal driving instructional and operational changes. Dr. Dance's cabinet and executive leaders were the first to begin racial equity leadership training in order to guide district leaders, school leaders, and staff in talking about equity, analyzing how policies and practices impacted students disparately, and removing barriers to increase opportunity. The Board of Education of Baltimore County became one of few across the country to adopt an equity policy under the recommendation of Dr. Dance.

Second, *breaking through persistent achievement* gaps required a positive culture and climate at every school while managing systemic change. Helping every student thrive required deeper relationships through more opportunities for meaningful student voice, mentoring, character education, and more support from school social workers and counselors. New investments in staff and leaders included career ladders and leadership preparation as well as school-based leadership opportunities outside of the classroom for excellent educators.

Third, accountability shifted from tracking average proficiency to *individual student growth* toward college and career readiness. Focusing on average proficiency did not challenge those students already above the performance standard and excluded those who grew but remained below the standard.

Fourth, Dr. Dance leveraged *meaningful use of* technology to personalize learning in such a diverse school system. Timely formative and summative measures enabled teachers to challenge students at their own level with consistent high standards guided by a digital curriculum in the core content areas and quality digital resources. Online classes provided access to the world's course catalog.

Despite fewer students demonstrating kindergarten readiness at school entry, young learners were catching up at a fast pace. More elementary students met reading and math growth targets each year as compared to 2014–2015 when 1:1 digital learning launched in elementary grades at S.T.A.T. (Students and Teachers Accessing Tomorrow) Lighthouse Schools before expanding to all elementary schools. In addition to devices, S.T.A.T. included digital curriculum; intensive training on enabling student ownership and engagement of learning; wireless and broadband infrastructure; and the BCPS One information portal for students, staff, and families.

Grade-level performance in both reading and mathematics had been strongest in Grades 1, 2, and 4. Grades 1 and 2 met or exceeded the national norms for mathematics by 2017. All elementary grades met or exceeded national norms for reading by 2017. In addition, teachers and students had been working hard to close gaps in reading by Grade 3. By winter 2017, more than 56 percent of Grade 3 students were outperforming their peers nationally in reading, as measured by the percent of students who scored at or above the 50th percentile.

To close the race-based graduation rate gap, system and school leaders were charged with making graduation a priority at every high school. This priority was reinforced through monthly accountability meetings and early warning systems at Grades 6 and 9. Onsite credit recovery was expanded to every high school with day, evening, and weekend options for first-ever maximum flexibility. Schools strengthened relationships with all students and used these relationships to customize dropout prevention committees in collaboration with struggling students and their families.

Taken together, during five short years, a focus on equity, culture, student growth, and the appropriate use of technology resulted in a deliberate, sustainable, and supported transformation in teaching and learning. Dr. Dance's ability to promote and deliver equity, implement and manage change, and impact and strategically communicate a systemic message were key drivers in BCPS being recognized as one of the best school systems in the country.

PREFACE

Life takes us to unexpected places sometimes.

The future is never set in stone, remember that.

—Erin Morgenstern

From my early years, I always wanted to be a corporate and civil rights attorney. It appears that a funny thing happened on my way to the courtroom: I stumbled upon a career trajectory that launched me into the atmosphere of educational administration and led to traveling my unbelievable journey to the superintendent's office and to assisting educational leaders throughout the country. In 1754, Horace Walpole coined the term *serendipity* to refer to an unexpected discovery of something made on the way to another destination. In his Persian fairy tale *The Three Princes of Serendip*, Walpole alludes to the phenomenon as that by which we are "always making discoveries, by accidents and sagacity, of things which they were not in quest of." I cannot think of a more suitable term to characterize the fortunate happenstance that catapulted me into my reality.

While in college, I volunteered my time to mentoring and tutoring male students in a local school system. One afternoon, a student named Brandon said to me, "I wish all teachers could be like you!" His words moved me, and with that, I hit the snooze button on becoming a lawyer and became a full-time teacher after I graduated from college.

For the longest time, it appeared I was on the "two-year path." I taught high school English for two years, served as a high school assistant principal for two years, served as a middle school principal for two years, served as an assistant superintendent for two years, served as a director for one year, and served as a chief school officer for two years before becoming the superintendent of Baltimore County Public Schools (BCPS). Ironically, I never really applied for any of these positions; I sort of fell into each.

My becoming superintendent made national news and circulated throughout the education community as being groundbreaking because I was only thirty years old; the average age of a district superintendent is significantly older. According to the American Association of School Administrators (AASA), the mean age of a superintendent is between fifty-four and fifty-five years of age, and only 6 percent of superintendents are minorities. Thus, the system's selection of a young African-American to take the reins of its over $1 billion budget and to oversee the education of more than 100,000 students—a considerably large school district by any standards—raised more than a few eyebrows.

During my career, I have developed a reputation for getting things done. Because of my commitment to understanding; connecting; and, most importantly, believing in people, I have come to be known for effecting change in a positive manner.

This commitment should be evident throughout this book, and it would prove to serve me well as superintendent in a large district that had been dealing with student demographic shifts, an aging infrastructure, and rising enrollment— elements germane to many school systems throughout the country. The system was also struggling to discover its next steps toward academic excellence. However, despite the need for change, the system was a good school system, and good school systems rarely deal well with change.

I remember a close colleague telling me that I could last for twelve years in the school system if I didn't "rock the boat." I also recall seeing on the conference room wall at the BCPS central office a framed quote by Jack Welch, which said, "When the rate of change in an organization falls behind the rate of change outside of an organization, the end is in sight." That quote has resonated strongly with me. Leaders, particularly in education, must ensure that the viability of the organization is clear and relevant in a rapidly changing economy. This is critical in education as virtually every other industry has evolved with the times, and our classrooms still look the same. Additionally, an organization's viability is evident through its people and customers.

When leaders are hired, a charge is usually given. In my case, I was hired for three reasons: to galvanize the community around the next level of academic excellence for all students, to develop and execute a comprehensive facilities plan in a district with chronically outdated school buildings, and to communicate a clear and succinct message.

The Board of Education did not want these changes only for certain segments of the community; they wanted these enhancements for every student in the county. From day one,

I appreciated the straightforwardness to address equity. Equity is a term that is frequently used but has various meanings depending on whom you ask. To me, equity means providing exactly what an individual needs to be successful. This involves leaders critically analyzing their organization's policies and practices to ensure that they do not disenfranchise certain employees or certain customers. Due to our nation's history, especially with segregation in schools, educators must ensure those practices don't further exacerbate the achievement gap that so prevails the conversation between different groups of students. In many cases, we've created these circumstances ourselves, and without bold and deliberate action, they will continue and in most instances get worse. During my administration, equity remained the solid principle I used for directing the school system, and it is the main strategy I believe leaders must embrace and hold true to ensure all students receive a quality education. Equity, however, must not be viewed as an add-on but, indeed, as my mentor, friend, and *New York Times* best-selling author Wes Moore notably calls "The Work."

What You Will Find in This Book

I have closely studied Abraham Lincoln's leadership as a model for my own. It was said that Lincoln's cabinet was filled with people who would challenge his thinking. When he initially spoke about an issue, he was well prepared since he had examined all potential perspectives on that topic. It is my hope that this book challenges your thinking to become a better leader regardless of your current level of employment. It is true that every new position will arrive with its own set of struggles, its own unique challenges, and the necessity of mastering a learning curve of the particulars. It is perfectly normal to struggle

> "It is my hope that this book challenges your thinking to become a better leader regardless of your current level of employment."

through these challenges until you gain a mastery of knowledge to be effective in the position. Know what you don't know.

Who This Book Is For

Leadership is tough, and I believe educational leaders hold some of the most complex positions in the world. My purpose is to help anyone I can to progress. To do this, I hold the unwavering belief that a commitment to establishing equity, to understanding change and the change management process, and to knowing how to communicate with various audiences must exist. I was always extremely dedicated and focused in every position I occupied. I believe success occurred due to one primary reason: my connection and belief in people. Throughout my career, people have sensed my loyalty, my sincerity, and my commitment. This is, in a large part, why I could be entrusted with other positions at higher levels and the responsibility to help so many others.

> "I hold the unwavering belief that a commitment to establishing equity, to understanding change and the change management process, and to knowing how to communicate . . . must exist."

Ultimately, the key principle that has driven my success as a leader boils down to one word:

people. Through an authentic connection with people, you can get *anything* done as a leader . . . *anything*! Once you learn to build relationships that allow you to effectively lead through people, you will become more effective at accomplishing those big goals. Many people fear the unknown, and change requires embarking on the unknown. *What will be the result of the change? What will it take to change? What will be the expense in time, comfort, and resources? What will be the impact of change?* People are naturally reluctant to take chances. However, when you learn to work effectively with people and you develop a productive method of guiding them through the process of change management, you demonstrate their need to embrace change and to play an active role in making your goal a reality. You can learn how to lead through people, you *can* learn how to effect organizational change, and you *can* accomplish great things. It merely takes mastering a few key principles that I can personally attest to being efficacious because of my own experience.

While primarily focused on education, I write this book for all who desire to excel in their field. I also wrote this book for anyone who endeavors to be an effective leader in any field. One of the most valuable lessons that I have learned through the course of my career is that leadership has universal qualities that govern all arenas. I write this book for anyone who is passionate about helping people, especially young people, develop and maximize their latent potential that lurks somewhere deep inside. It is my hope that everyone who reads the words on these pages will understand that the term *leader* is not about merely having a title. Finally, my hope is that this book will play a key role in fostering two things that are desperately needed to advance education: an increase in the number of female leaders and an increase in the number of leaders of color.

I have been fortunate to have stumbled upon the greatest career in the world: that of providing a quality education for the next generation of students who will be our future leaders and global citizens and of supporting dedicated leaders committed to the same goal. Best of all, I'm going to navigate this process with you in the same way that I have navigated through each phase of my career: by having fun and enjoying every moment of it.

Know that you are a leader and can impact positive change. A whole generation of students is depending on you to become the best educational leader you can possibly be, so prepare yourself to be challenged, and let's grow together!

ACKNOWLEDGMENTS

Cherish your human connections:

Your relationships with family and friends.

—Barbara Bush

For five years, I was extremely fortunate to serve as the superintendent of Baltimore County Public Schools (BCPS) in Towson, Maryland, which is located adjacent to the city of Baltimore. Those years were by far the best of my professional life. I led the organization from my heart, believing that we could move mountains, and while not literally, we began tackling some large complex issues, which will take time, effort, energy, and commitment to realize its full impact. The strides we made, which garnered us numerous national, state, and local awards, were due to the dedication of our teachers, principals, staff, parents, community leaders, and especially our students who rose to the high standards we set for them each day. As this book is about three main areas of my work as superintendent, I want to personally take the opportunity to thank the entire Team BCPS family for everything you did and continue to do for the students of Baltimore County.

To my senior leadership team in Baltimore County, including my wonderful assistant, Brenda: Words cannot express how thankful I am to each of you for your support and commitment as we led the work of transforming teaching and learning for over 112,000 students in an extraordinary short period of time. You believed in me, and I will always believe in each of you.

We are all where we are due to caring mentors: Thank you to Dr. Freeman Hrabowski, Wes Moore, Dr. Bill Hite, Dr. Terry Grier, Dr. Deborah Pettit, Dr. Mark Edwards, and Dr. Marcus Newsome for providing guidance to me preparing me for my life's work.

To my editor, Linda Nicholson: You have always been there when I needed you and for that I say thank you! You helped me bring this book to life, and I am excited to share it with the world.

To the New Psalmist Baptist Church family led by Bishop Walter Scott Thomas Sr.: Thank you for providing me support and encouragement during my time in Baltimore.

And last but certainly not least, to my family and friends: Thank you for always supporting me. To my mother, Leatrice; my son who is my pride and joy, Myles Dallas; my father, Roy; my sister, Khesia; and my closest friends, Tommi, Ingrid, Desiree, Terrell, Rakeem, Regina, James, JBG3, and the Council: I love each of you, and I could not have accomplished this or the work without each of you being you!

Publisher's Acknowledgments

Corwin gratefully acknowledges the contributions of the following reviewers:

Tanna Nicely, Principal
South Knoxville Elementary
Knoxville, TN

LaQuita Outlaw, Principal, Grades 6–8
Bay Shore Middle School
Bay Shore, NY

Kathy Rhodes, Principal
Hinton Elementary
Hinton, IA

Veronica Rodriguez, Special Education Coordinator
Chester W. Nimitz Middle School
Huntington Park, CA

ABOUT THE AUTHOR

Internationally renowned educator and speaker, **Dr. S. Dallas Dance** envisions and leads change that creates opportunities for all young people—including students of color and those living in poverty—to thrive as critical thinkers, thoughtful leaders, and lifelong learners. His calling is motivating teams of all sizes to develop young minds and working with leaders and organizations to build capacity to do greater work for all of the individuals within their community.

Numerous national awards and board appointments—from institutions including the White House, Microsoft, and ASCD—recognize his impact on organizational culture, rigorous instruction, vibrant leadership pathways, leveraging technology, and dynamic community engagement.

Dr. Dance is the president and chief executive officer of The DDance Group, an organization focused on partnering with clients to improve strategic outcomes. Clients have included public and private schools, school districts, government agencies, and associations, and businesses. Prior to starting The DDance Group, Dr. Dance served as the superintendent of Baltimore County Public Schools (BCPS) in Maryland with over 112,000 students, 173 schools, and over 21,000 employees. As leader of the nation's 25th largest school system, Dance pioneered equity-centered shifts in teaching and learning to close the graduation achievement gap between black and white students, while increasing diploma rates overall.

Prior to his appointment in Baltimore County, Dr. Dance served as one of three chief school officers responsible for the administration of nearly 300 schools in the Houston Independent School District, the seventh largest school system in the nation. Before his tenure in Houston, Dr. Dance served in executive leadership positions in Virginia that leveraged his expertise in curriculum, instruction, assessment, school improvement, and strategic planning.

Dance earned a doctoral degree in educational leadership and a master's degree in administration and supervision from Virginia Commonwealth University. His bachelor's degree in English is from Virginia Union University.

Dr. Dance enjoys traveling and reading as well as music and all sports, especially golf. He is the proud father of one son, Myles Dallas Dance.

INTRODUCTION

Success occurs when opportunity meets preparation.

—Zig Ziglar

As I sat at the end of a huge rectangular table in a large oval room, which appeared to be as large as the stadium home of the Baltimore Ravens, I was preparing myself for my new reality. With six microphones in front of me and seven editors seated on all sides of me, I was about to be grilled by the editorial board of the *Baltimore Sun*.

As the questions commenced, sweat soaked my undershirt, and I was thankful that the perspiration did not show on my face.

A softball question was thrown: "Dr. Dance, has it hit you yet?"

"Yes, sir! It most certainly has," I responded.

"Now, let's get to the meat and potatoes," one of the editors said.

I gulped.

"You're relatively young for such a huge position. Are you worried?" asked another editor.

"I am not worried," I said. "I am humble enough to know what I don't know and inquisitive enough to learn what I need to know."

"What's been the biggest eye-opener for you in the past few weeks?" the head editor inquired.

It was at that point that I allowed the voice of the community to speak to the editorial board, and from that moment, I used that voice to shape my leadership principles as the superintendent of Baltimore County Public Schools (BCPS), one of the largest school systems in America.

I took a sip of water and spoke from my heart.

"I've met countless parents, students, employees, and community members who are concerned about two main things: the widening division between the haves and have-nots. We cannot allow this to continue in our county," I said. "Additionally, many stakeholders highlight the quality of our school system but due to conceived complacency are concerned that we are not positioning ourselves to ensure our success in the future, which will require us to change and manage change purposefully."

"What are you going to do about it?" another editor asked.

"Use my communication skills as much as humanly possible to make, as John Kotter (2012) put it, 'the status quo more dangerous than the unknown,'" I replied.

For nearly ninety minutes, the intense exchange would continue with me centering my words around principles of equity, change management, and communication. At the end, the head editor said to me, "It appears you sure are consistent."

It also appeared that I survived it, but on the drive back to my office, one thought hit me like a ton of bricks: YOU HAVE A HUGE RESPONSIBILITY! YOU ARE NOW THE SUPERINTENDENT, AND YOU MUST DELIVER.

When I stepped down as the superintendent after five years, I had no professional regrets. While there was much more work to be done, our system achieved considerable success. In a fiscally conservative environment that had not raised taxes in over a quarter of a century, we undertook more than $200 million in instructional initiatives. Our elementary school students began to learn Spanish. We had a graduation rate of nearly 90 percent, the highest graduation rate in the history of the school system and an exceptional one for a school system of our magnitude. In fact, ours was among the few particularly large school systems in the country to close statistically the achievement gap between white and black students. There were more students reading on grade level and more students taking the SAT, a barrier to college admission for many students of color and students who are living in poverty, due to the opportunity we provided for all high school juniors to test during the school day FREE. Another point of progress, one of which I am particularly proud, is that every decision we made was from an equity standpoint.

> ". . . ours was among the few particularly large school systems in the country to statistically close the achievement gap between white and black students."

Because we dared to have bold conversations pertaining to race, which, in many cases, exacerbates the achievement gap, we made significant progress toward significantly raising expectations for all students and eliminating the achievement gap. And we openly spoke about race and class and eliminating barriers—unapologetically spoke about it and addressed it—even though it was tough. Lastly, we all know an organization's culture can derail its mission if it does not focus on productivity and the people in need of its services. Consequently, I was proud that our school administration's culture was rooted in the teamwork of working together on behalf of all students. *All* truly meant all for the team, and I modeled it daily.

> "I am particularly proud . . . that every decision we made was from an equity standpoint."

Overall, we produced some remarkable changes at an accelerated rate that was at least three to four times faster than the average rate of change for a system of our nature and size. The changes that we made captured the attention of educators across the world, including South Korea and Beijing. In fact, every year, we had dozens of school systems request visits to see what we were doing and how we managed to accomplish so much in such a short amount of time. We also received numerous accolades and awards and the unwavering support of our elected officials who represented both major political parties but who rallied together for schools as I frequently used the pulpit of the superintendency to discuss the economic impact of great schools on communities.

My leadership story has not been without its challenges, however, and I share several of them in the subsequent pages, particularly through "The Principle in Action . . ." sections. But my journey does extend itself to presently offering help to others, other leaders who want to make it—meaning the work—happen. This is my passion and my purpose. My passion for helping other leaders achieve similar success solidified as I listened to a speech by U.S. congressman Elijah Cummings. Speaking in downtown Baltimore shortly after the 2015 unrest, he said, "We are proud of Dallas for his work in providing strong educational leadership to our region, state, and nation, but we need more Dallases who can provide leadership to more children! We need strong leadership!" His words made me realize that I needed to push myself to help more people understand that rising to positions of leadership is completely possible. My aim is to encourage other leaders with potential to seek positions that I had occupied and to help them further once they reach their goal—growing more leaders. This is my passion and purpose.

LEADING FOR EQUITY

FOCUSING ON EACH CHILD, EVERY DAY

Fairness does not mean everyone gets the same.

Fairness means everyone gets what they need.

—Rick Riordan

Know What Your Values Are

Roy Disney, an American businessman and cofounder of the Walt Disney Company, once said, "It's not hard to make decisions when you know what your values are." The very first step toward success as a leader is recognizing your personal values. Having an intimate level of awareness of your own ethics will help you understand why you make your decisions and why you act as you do. There are numerous life experiences that serve to shape our particular values. We use these values as leaders in our day-to-day interactions with supervisors, colleagues, direct reports, and others. Subsequently, being cognizant of the values held by those with whom you work is also essential.

The Haves and the Have Nots

When I was a teacher and part-time administrator, I was frequently given student discipline cases. One memorable case involved two football players who got into a fight. Obviously, fighting is unacceptable and consequences must occur. However, I believe one of the primary roles of an administrator in situations like this is to the teach students about acceptable behavior. In this case, I didn't want to avoid consequences, and since I did want to ensure another fight wouldn't occur, conflict resolution was in order. Ultimately, having the students talk out their differences worked, and then it was time for discipline. I imposed the mandatory suspension for fighting for both students: ten days. It was harsh, yes, but back then there was zero tolerance for fighting. Nonetheless, parents of one of the students were friends with a school board member, and as luck would have it, that student didn't serve his suspension at all because a high-ranking district official became involved. The other student, however, served all ten days. I was obviously livid. At the time, one of my colleagues said it was a race issue, as one student was white and the other black. While race could have played a factor, what I know for sure is the situation wasn't handled with equity. Honestly, since it was resolved, I would have been fine with no suspension and an emphasis on community service.

Three months later, I met this high-ranking district official, and within two minutes of being around the individual and hearing him talk disrespectfully about students and adults, I clearly recognized why he did what he did for one student and not the other. In hindsight, I still wonder with an attitude like his how he was able to make sound decisions for *all* students. Although this wasn't the only one of my cases that was overturned, I wouldn't allow future reversals of my decisions to bother me because I took the time to learn the value set of individuals involved and further deepened my own.

Lessons Learned

- First, this experience made me question zero-tolerance policies. Missing two weeks of school has a severe effect on a student's academic success.

- It also made me realize that we must always be mindful of how race can inject itself into schools and cause major gaps from academics to discipline.

- Most importantly, it reinforced for me how important it is for leaders to be grounded not only in equity but in values, too. ●

I have never allowed myself to grow upset with leaders' decisions because I have always taken the time to try to understand them by listening to them and watching their actions. When you recognize their values and beliefs, you realize how they think, how they act, and how they respond. In other words, everything that they do is an expectation, not a surprise.

Our values define what we believe and who we are. Thus, if we are to be effective as leaders, our ethics must be in alignment with the types of ideals that bring success because we lead with our values and beliefs. Regardless of how many books we read, how many conferences we attend, how many mentors we seek for guidance and direction, or how much willpower we exert to do things differently, without values, our efforts will be exercises in futility. Our actions will not change unless our beliefs change, and our beliefs will not change unless our values change.

Demonstrate a Strong Appreciation for People

There are certain moral convictions that a leader must possess, especially in education. The primary must-have is this: a strong appreciation for people. This value is characterized by the belief that people—all people, young-old, rich-poor, all races, all ethnicities—matter. This simply is the meaning of equity and equity in action, as we can't focus on equity without appreciating all people. In the case of educators and students, I sum this up to leaders with a clear takeaway of this: Ensure you are making the decision on behalf of all children in the same vein you would make it if it were your own child. This standard raises the bar, which is where it should be.

> "Ensure you are making the decision on behalf of all children in the same vein you would make it if it were your own child. This standard raises the bar, which is where it should be."

Former U.S. secretary of state and retired four-star general in the U.S. Army Colin Powell, who undoubtedly knew a thing or two about success, once said, "Leadership is about people, not programs." I could not agree more, and I often shared this philosophy wherever I went and frequently reinforced it with my principals. I still share this quote.

When we hold a genuine sense of value for people, we appreciate them for their unique qualities and for what they offer, and we are compelled to hold them in high regard simply because their lives matter as fellow human beings. When it comes to leadership, valuing people is a necessary first step toward treating all people with equity.

My entire career has been spent focusing on how to treat people equitably and fairly to accomplish a goal. Consequently, any leader who will succeed in working with people must also operate and lead from a perspective that recognizes equity.

Most educational leaders are trained to think in terms of equality—everyone receives the *same* treatment, the *same*

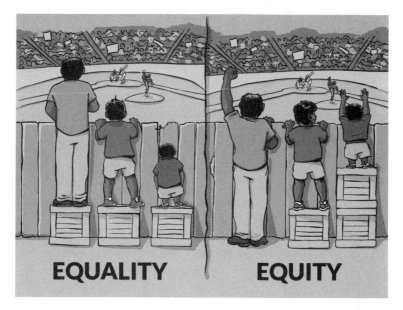

EQUALITY   **EQUITY**

Source: Interaction Institute for Social Change | Artist: Angus Maguire.

resources, and the *same* opportunities. Equality engenders a
sense that someone must "lose" for others to gain because
you cannot make people equal. However, equity is different.
When we operate through an equity lens, we ensure every
single person with whom we interact, whether it be a
student, teacher, or employee, is given exactly what he
or she needs to be successful. Consequently, because this
might not be the same for each person, it varies from the
concept of equality. A simple example I have heard several
colleagues use is equality is when you ensure all students
have a pair of shoes; whereas, equity is when you ensure
all students have a pair of shoes that fit. This essentially
guarantees that each student gets exactly what he or she
needs to have his or her needs met.

Equity Means Putting People First

One of my newer principals was frustrated by some of his teachers who were late arriving to work. Every day, each was ten minutes late, and he believed he needed to "set a strong example" that tardiness wasn't going to be tolerated on his watch. This lateness had been going on for almost a month when the ambitious principal finally issued letters of reprimand to the teachers. When the principal's supervisor became involved, it was discovered that one of the teachers was going through a tumultuous divorce and was essentially homeless. Because a colleague was picking her up each morning and dropping off her daughter at a nearby school, both teachers were tardy. When this came to my attention, we worked with the principal to ensure both teachers had the adequate coverage and allowed the one teacher's daughter to attend the same school as her mom. This was also our teachable moment with the ambitious principal.

Lesson Learned

- You must know and value your people as human beings with personal circumstances that will have an impact on professional situations. The scenario that was just given is not the resolution needed for every situation, but without an equity lens, we would not have been able to support that teacher based on her current needs. However, by doing so she has become one of our strongest supporters. ●

My experience at the central office level, both in Texas and Maryland, grounded me further in equity. The school district in Texas was large and complex with its 90 percent student population of color and 80 percent population living in poverty. Before my colleagues and I arrived, the district had been making pivotal decisions based on a student's race or zip code.

This led to heartbreaking and noticeable inequities between students in the more prosperous zip codes and those in the less prosperous. To address this disparity, Dr. Terry Grier, the system's superintendent (known as one of the boldest, most assertive superintendents), assembled our team. We then shifted our focus to equity, grounding our work in moving all our students forward without regard for race or socioeconomic standing. The team was unapologetic about addressing race and poverty to approach equity, and to be honest, many members of our community, including teachers, parents, students, business leaders, and elected officials, were pleased that our actions matched our words.

Over the span of my career, I have learned and embraced some critical considerations about equity.

● ● ● ● TIPS FOR LEADERS ON ESTABLISHING EQUITY

Equity takes leadership.

Equity requires preparing for resistance.

Equity is about more than race.

Equity is the work, not an add-on to the work.

Equity is what students want us to focus on and are demanding it.

Addressing Equity Takes Leadership

Discussions of equity are especially relevant and important in today's schools. According to the National Center for Education Statistics, there are almost 14,000 school systems, nearly 100,000 public schools, and more than 50 million students in

> "When we do not move forward with equity to ensure a high-quality education for all children, we all lose on the district, state, and national levels."

the United States. Nearly half of these students are students of color, and nearly half of all students qualify for free or reduced-price meals and are on the losing side of a widening achievement gap. Based on reading, math, and graduation statistics, their nonminority peers are outpacing. Without an established sense of equity in all schools and in all districts across the nation, an increasingly smaller segment of students will receive a higher-quality education, while many other students will receive an inferior education that will not adequately prepare them to live successful lives as global citizens. More than anything, the lack of equity in education will affect our local and national economies and the nation's GDP. Why? Because those receiving an inferior education will be ill equipped to occupy many jobs that call for levels of advanced skills, particularly in STEM (science, technology, engineering, and math)-related subjects. This will inevitably leave a void in the marketplace. When we do not move forward with equity to ensure a high-quality education for all children, we all lose on the district, state, and national levels.

●●● THE PRINCIPLE IN ACTION

Too Important Not to Address

When I first started equity work as a superintendent, a superintendent colleague asked me why I was addressing this issue. This individual had worked in the school system before, and he strongly believed the system was not ready for such a strong dialogue or work around the topic, especially since based on his experience it was clearly going to be a conversation around race. He advised to "give it some time."

I remember asking the question, "When is the right time?"

The reply was, "No time soon! You're going to get yourself fired!"

My response was, "We are leaving students behind, and it is not only African-American students. It is also poor students and students with disabilities. While I have to be strategic, not addressing this simply is *not* an option."

Naturally, I got an unpleasant look.

Lesson Learned

- Leaders have to lead and can't get comfortable. Leaders should be bold and take risks based on relevant student achievement data. If the data points to a difficult topic needing to be addressed, use the data as your guide. I do not know more relevant and powerful data than achievement gaps, which exist in the majority of our schools, but they don't exist by race alone. ●

In many cases, equity is not a naturally occurring quality that emerges on its own in our school systems. As nearly every other industry has evolved, our educational system remains largely the same as it has been for centuries, which stratifies students into groups and in essence can exacerbate achievement and opportunity gaps as opposed to ameliorating both. Therefore, as educators, we must disrupt the system and promote equity and opportunity for all children by focusing deliberately on the needs of all students, especially students who have traditionally not performed as well as their peers. Equity will be present only if leaders understand its importance, which means valuing their students enough to advocate for equity on their behalf, to bring it to the table, and engage in efforts to make it a reality for them.

In order to stand out as an equity leader, you must be willing to ask yourself some tough questions: What is it that every single student in my school or district needs to be successful? What is it that every single employee needs to be successful? Once you have answered these questions and built relationships with your community to ensure their awareness of their children's issues, create precise strategies that will help you actualize your goals, focusing solely on student academic outcomes, and remember that students' needs can be met only if employees have the capacity to ensure that the students receive personalized and specific attention. This can be done!

I was intentional about building the case for equity as a school superintendent. During my tenure, I wrote an op-ed published in the local newspaper expressing the need for the work, and the response was great.

"BALTIMORE COUNTY STUDENTS DESERVE EQUITY"

by S. Dallas Dance

The Baltimore Sun
November 22, 2015

I began my tenure as superintendent of Baltimore County Public Schools (BCPS) by listening to voices from all across the region during the 2012–2013 school year. From coastal to rural and suburban neighborhoods, this advice from students, families, educators and the community formed the foundation of our five-year strategic plan.

From many voices came a common concern: inequity. Stakeholders questioned differences in student access to academic rigor, resources including technology and modern facilities. Our high average student performance masked gaps in achievement between student groups based on race, ethnicity, gender, income level, special education status and English proficiency.

To interrupt these patterns, the Blueprint 2.0: Our Way Forward strategic plan is focused on graduating each and every one of our students globally competitive and prepared to thrive in the knowledge economy. We cannot let demographics continue to predict our students' performance, especially as our growing enrollment becomes increasingly diverse. Students of color now comprise 57.9 percent of our enrollment, with 47.4 percent of our students eligible for free or reduced-price meals. To put that percentage in perspective, BCPS has more students eligible for free or reduced-price meals than are enrolled in D.C. Public Schools. That is today's Baltimore County student population. Additionally, students speak almost 90 languages from more than 100 countries.

As we move forward, ensuring that each of our students has equitable access to an effective digital learning environment and second language proficiency, as called for in our Theory of Action, could not rest solely on the able shoulders of the BCPS Office of Equity and Cultural Proficiency. Instead, our task was to truly build capacity across the organization to expand opportunity for every student, increase academic rigor in every classroom, and eliminate troubling achievement gaps, which in many cases are race-based.

As the first leaders engaged in the BCPS equity transformation in summer 2013, the Board of Education of Baltimore County then

(Continued)

(Continued)

set the foundation for systemic equity through Board policy 0100. This landmark policy affirms that "disparities on the basis of race, special education status, gender, ethnicity, sexual orientation, English language learner (ELL) status or socio-economic status are unacceptable and are directly at odds with the belief that all students can achieve."

To make good on this promise, we began and are continuing to implement a three-phase equity plan supported by training for district and school leaders and staff: (1) developing a shared language for discussing racial equity, (2) coaching for racial equity and (3) putting equity into practice. Applying an equity lens is our way of removing obstacles to student progress by analyzing how beliefs, policies and practices differentially impact students. Every school examines the root causes of their achievement gaps through an equity-focused School Progress Plan.

Instructionally, we are creating learner-centered environments that personalize and customize learning to provide equity, giving each student what he or she needs to achieve high academic outcomes. This transformation is extremely hard work. However, we are seeing huge gains. Our classrooms are now alive with movement, visuals, and sound to help all students develop needed creativity, communication, collaboration and critical thinking skills.

Teachers guide flexible small groups, advise students working on their own and provide one-on-one instruction. Furniture is strategically arranged to allow these seamless transitions. Students are empowered with the responsibility to choose how to engage with content and how to demonstrate what they have learned.

Technology is a key leverage tool for facilitating learner-centered environments across the district. Through S.T.A.T., or Students and Teachers Accessing Tomorrow, educators are using a dynamic digital curriculum and materials. The BCPS One online portal helps teachers organize flexible groups and assignments and facilitates easy parent and student access to grades, assignments and added communication.

All of our elementary schools and seven middle schools have placed 1:1 devices in students' hands to better engage and motivate learners. These Lighthouse schools are systemwide at Grades 1 through 3, schoolwide at last year's 10 pilot elementary schools and in Grade 6 at this year's pilot middle schools.

A self-paced online program is supplementing fourth grade Spanish instruction at 25 Passport schools to give our students the advantages of second language proficiency by graduation. Last year's 10 pilot schools have begun Spanish at grade five. We're learning from the careful roll out of Lighthouse and Passport schools in order to expand these opportunities to every student.

Parents of more than 111,000 students are choosing Baltimore County Public Schools, and we are expecting additional growth over the next decade. We owe it to each student to guide our decisions with equity, meeting students where they are, ensuring their growth and preparing them for success in the future.

Our students deserve equity. Let's continue innovating to get students at every school, all across the county, off to the best possible start. Their futures are in our hands.

Every organization can change and embrace equity because the stakes are too high to justify balking. It's the leader's responsibility, however, to work purposefully and tactically to persuade as many people as possible to raise their expectations, both internally and externally. In some situations, this task might be easier to achieve than in others, but I know from personal experience that it is never impossible. I was a young man when I worked in a small rural school district where there were about 300 black students in a system of 6,000 students, and I embarked on a plan to promote an agenda of equity. There were gaps in that district's practices based on race and poverty, and these gaps were addressed and corrected. When I worked in a large urban district, 90 percent of the students were of color, and the school system faced the challenge of promoting equity. Although my initial conversation with the system's leaders started with addressing basic needs for students living in poverty—that is, those who needed food and shelter—the conversation extended to how we needed to adequately fund schools or equalize access to our magnet programs to ensure a level playing field throughout the districts. Both the rural and urban situations addressed equity in very specific ways based on local context but driven by student academic outcomes. In both contexts, my colleagues and I had to be equally strategic. I had to build a case in both environments to create awareness to ensure students, teachers, and employees had everything that they needed to ensure growth, and I had to depend on data to tell the story. As it was driven by local context, to ensure students got what they needed to be successful, this ranged from home Internet access being provided for students in rural areas to community school models being developed for students in urban areas. Due to much of my experience being in suburban and urban school systems, a combination of both as well as extended learning time became a priority. Nonetheless, as I personally know how hard the work of establishing equity can be, I thoroughly enjoy the work of assisting school and district leaders to develop strategic plans and deliberate actions addressing this huge rock.

Addressing Equity
Will Guarantee Resistance

This is not easy work. A thorough understanding of the gaps in achievement databased on all student groups and a deliberate plan for building the case for awareness and buy-in are essential to success because when leaders attempt to lead their schools or districts with a sense of equity, there will undoubtedly be pushback. Typically, opposition to equity initiatives arises from those who mistakenly feel that equity is simply a race issue. This is because when educators discuss the gaps that exist in achievement, the gap is usually viewed as a gap between black students and white students. Although race can be the primary driver—and in most cases is—it is not the only force in issues of equity. As this depends on the student achievement data that exist within the school and district context, the leader must ensure these data are highlighted from multiple angles, including race, gender, socioeconomic status, special education, and English language learners to name a few. Ultimately, while it could boil down to being a race issue, if the leader simply leaves it as a race issue without quantifiable data speaking to the specific gap area, it could lead to people being dismissive altogether. Additionally, in some cases, without the specific gap area, a community could tend to take a path of least resistance—that is, wanting to focus on students living in poverty as opposed to a particular race when the data are clear it is a race issue.

Instead, the leader must start with effectively building a collective sense of awareness for *what* equity truly is and *why* equity is necessary, and he or she must establish a case for *how* equity can be feasibly and successfully implemented for the benefit of *all* students involved. It must be clear that no one has to lose in order to address issues of equity. Be bold in tackling equity as a community. Even initial opponents to equity can be convinced of the need for change by a leader who takes the time to strategically build a solid case. A simple statistic on the number of white students living in poverty can be an eye-opener. While it is easy to passionately burst in with ideas, take the time to build a case. A lawyer never goes into the courtroom without a solid case, and we should not approach this issue without one either.

●●● THE PRINCIPLE IN ACTION

Together We Achieve More

I frequently mentor new administrators, and one of my mentees had just been promoted to a middle school principal position in a small suburban district and wanted to tackle equity. When he mentioned his thoughts to his supervisor, she immediately thought about race. However, in his 750-student school, which was split fifty-fifty with white students and African-American students, he saw bigger achievement gaps based on poverty. Three months into his position, he noticed that his students on free or reduced-price meals were not achieving the same level of learning as their peers, and he wanted to make immediate changes. As leaders, we know that where we place our fiscal resources reflects where our priorities lie. Therefore, when he hastily began changing student schedules and moving money to various areas of need within his budget in order to tackle the issue, he met resistance from his internal and external communities regarding *what* he was doing and *why* he was doing it. He was well intentioned, but he soon recognized that his approach was wrong. He called me, and we worked out a plan to address the resistance. He created a school improvement team whose primary responsibility involved analyzing data, researching solutions, and recommending actions. Through their work, the team ended up recommending the same solutions he had initially proposed. Because the team (made up of school employees and community members) proposed the ideas, the larger community was more willing to endorse them. This was a win-win! As my late grandmother would always say, "There is no telling how far we can get as long as we don't care who gets the credit." That former mentee is now an assistant superintendent.

Lessons Learned

- In leadership positions, we oftentimes feel we have to tackle everything ourselves. However, if we want the work to go well, we have to empower the team to help us seek solutions to the organization's problems.

- Initiatives are much more likely to be sustained if everyone has a role in the solution.

- As the African proverb states, "If you want to go fast, go alone. If you want to go far, go together." ●

When faced with resistance to an equity agenda, the average leader might succumb to the pressures. Maybe this is because people may believe it's an agenda focused solely on race or because people seem content with the status quo or because the change may be too controversial or because the local politics may appear to get in the way. To "keep the peace," the average leader might consider the resistance too burdensome and not want to address it. I get it, but the stakes are simply too high not to address it; it must be addressed responsibly and strategically. Therefore, it is your responsibility to promote what is right and what is fair for all students, not what is comfortable. As leaders, we must have vision. We must believe in the ability to look ahead and see how the leadership of today will transport our organizations during the next five, ten, and twenty years. This is where equity comes in as all organizations' customers, especially school system clients—our students—are rapidly changing.

●●● THE PRINCIPLE IN ACTION

Preparing Before the Crisis

In April 2015, the nation tuned in to the news media to see civic unrest in the city of Baltimore. Disturbing images flashed across television screens worldwide of black youth walking out of schools, looting, committing violent acts, destroying property, setting fires, and throwing rocks at the police. I remember looking at the visuals on CNN and MSNBC and thinking, *This is how the world is going to think of Baltimore from now on.* The reality is that the young people shown on television represented a very small percentage of Baltimore's population. However, because images in the media shape the perceptions that people deem to be reality, in the minds of viewers all over the world, Baltimore was a city of unrest overrun by violent black youth.

I was greatly saddened by these events and took the situation very personally. The levels of responsibility that we educators had in the matter occurred to me at the moment I realized that we, as adults, had cultivated—either directly or indirectly—some of the disturbing behaviors that our students were showcasing that day. Seeing these events unfold before me reaffirmed that Baltimore had a long way to go in how we dealt with issues of race, poverty, and hope.

The next day, the city of Baltimore closed its schools. (Baltimore City Public Schools and Baltimore County Public Schools [BCPS] are two separate school systems. I served as superintendent of the latter.) What was happening in the city of Baltimore could have easily happened in Baltimore County. However, we had no issues because we had already

24 Deliberate Excellence | Three Fundamental Strategies

spent the previous years focusing on leading with equity through conversation and action. While we took some pushback from regional leaders outside of Baltimore County, I was more than confident that the right decision was made. However, I became more focused on continuing the equity work, as it was the work and in forging a deeper relationship with the leadership of Baltimore City Public Schools to help address matters of race and equity through new school solutions and collaborative training efforts. My goal was to improve the future of all students within the Baltimore region even though several well-respected people told me repeatedly to "focus on the county's students; the city's students are not our responsibility." However, my passion was the region and equity being the work.

Lessons Learned

- If you haven't experienced a crisis or a tough situation, it will come. However, you want to make sure you are prepared before it arrives.

- All members of society need to feel a deep sense of hope—especially our children—and educators play a huge part in that. Without hope, children won't be able to see a bright future for themselves.

- Educators should not insulate students from tough conversations. In a democratic society, students must feel that school leaders are providing a safe space for them to voice their opinions and listening to the opinions of others to frame a balanced perspective. •

When leaders dare to face the resistance and advocate for equity, it is because we are driven by the mission to improve educational outcomes for all students. We recognize that when all students are educated, the community benefits—the story of strong communities. It is no secret that there has been a conspicuous achievement gap in our nation's schools, and this gap is a directional one that is a liability to certain students within our schools. What is not as conspicuous is the gaps in

> To eliminate these gaps, leaders must approach their work from a full-circle equity standpoint and intentionally develop local awareness and a local plan of action.

achievement that also exist in our educational system based on social class, gender, learning disabilities, language status, and so on. Remember that race may begin the conversation, but it can't end with race. To eliminate these gaps, leaders must approach their work from a full-circle equity standpoint and intentionally develop local awareness and a local plan of action.

The work is tough, and while I am disheartened at the gaps, I am hopeful and convinced that with a deep reflection of our values and with collective leadership from our communities, these gaps can be erased. We will get there!

Equity Is the Work, Not an "Add-on" to the Work

When speaking with other leaders, I often notice that as soon as the word *equity* arises in the conversation, we then hear, "I have so much on my plate already!" or "I simply do not have the time to address such a huge topic." Leaders who think like this view equity as an add-on to their work. However, we must understand that equity *is* the *work*! When leaders approach equity from this perspective, the work of addressing equity only gets in the way of what they perceive to be their "real" work, and it will only result in frustration without tangible results. Ask yourself the following: How will this decision impact "all" students? or Will this decision move toward eliminating or exacerbating our achievement gap?

Both questions are examples of equity work in action. This is instructional leadership at its core.

To effectively accomplish the work before you, you must hone your skills and learn how to build awareness for equity by building a case for it that no one can resist. The key is to deeply analyze your student data from all perspectives. Are more females graduating than males? Are more Latino/a students reading at grade level than black students? Are we suspending more students with disabilities than other students? Leaders can use these hard statistics as a flashlight (rather than a hammer) to begin to bring about the awareness that something needs to be done. This also allows us to put faces on the numbers: someone's son or someone's daughter. If we are honest, all schools and school districts have achievement gaps, so let's do something about them.

●●● THE PRINCIPLE IN ACTION

Knowing the Data and Root Cause

School systems must take a comprehensive approach if they desire to address equity. Each individual school's work toward equity must be grounded in its continuous improvement plan, and in order to eliminate confusion and frustration, there should be only one plan.

As a central office administrator, I spent hours focusing on equity when devising the school improvement planning process in which schools were required to identify and address the root cause of why equity goals were not being met. For example, a veteran school leader was reviewing her building's reading data and found that over the prior three school years fourth-grade students who qualified for

(Continued)

(Continued)

free or reduced-price meals were reading on a level averaging almost twenty-five points below their peers. Instead of crafting an arbitrary goal to assist the students who were behind, the key was to discern why this differential existed and then create an equity-based plan that would improve the students' reading skills, increase the scores, and meet the goal. The principal asked her school improvement team, "Why is it that each year our fourth-grade students living in poverty are scoring 25 percent less than their peers?" The top four or five reasons were listed on a fishbone diagram, and then the principal "drilled down" to discover the "why" for each reason. This continued until the improvement team focused on how the school could control solving for the issue within its control. In this case, the team discovered the struggling students were receiving less time overall in reading instruction since it was occurring first thing in the morning, and the students were in the cafeteria eating breakfast. Immediately, the school began a Breakfast in the Classroom program, which allowed the students to not miss classroom time each morning and thereby gaining ten minutes of additional reading instruction daily. Over the course of a 180-day school year, this equated to 1,800 additional minutes—the equivalent of over four additional school days. Within one year, the scores for fourth-grade students living in poverty were within 7 percentage points of their peers.

Lessons Learned

- Asking ourselves tough questions focusing on underperforming groups is addressing equity.

- The continuous improvement plan is the best weapon a school or school district has to address equity and meet goals.

- Unless leaders get to the root cause of why goals are not being met for all students, specific action steps to move the data cannot be taken. ●

As leaders, we feel really good when we meet our goals, and it is ultimately your job as a leader to reposition the concept of equity as a necessary motive to realize the goals people *sincerely* desire to see manifested for all children. As shown in the previously given example, positive results can occur when we focus specific actions to address equity goals for all students.

The nineteenth century educator and politician Horace Mann made the unwavering argument that "education is best provided in schools embracing children of all religious, social, and ethnic backgrounds." Mann's quote is the root of why equity is the work. As mentioned before, the nation's schools are changing demographically. In 2012, the Center for Public Education updated its report titled "The United States of Education: The Changing Demographics of the United States and Their Schools." In the report, it discusses how no one racial or ethnic group makes up a majority of the country's population. The report further details how schools are increasingly growing with the number of students of color, and as gaps continue to exist, a need to address equity will be paramount. I have always believed that a quality education is the one singular apparatus we can use to lift individuals out of poverty. I am an example of how through a quality education, I am making a better life for myself and my family. We all want this for all of our children regardless of whatever student groups that they fall into. This is why equity is our work.

Students Want Us to Focus on Equity, Not Equality

Race is simply not an issue with most children. From personal experiences, inside and outside of the classroom, I have learned that adults, not children, are the only ones primarily concerned with issues surrounding race. However, students learn to be biased when they hear what others (fellow students and adults) say and do.

As a teacher, school-based administrator, and central office administrator, I've seen students and heard students discuss at great lengths what they perceive to be significant inequities that exist. It is our job to take those voices to enact change that ultimately proves to benefit them while they are in our care and lasting well beyond.

●●● THE PRINCIPLE IN ACTION

Students Telling Their Story

We periodically had students dine with us prior to school board meetings. At one meeting, a board member made a couple of comments about how *equity* was a buzzword. He continued to say the teachers cared about all students. Shortly after making these comments, the board member, who was a former teacher, and the remaining members left the room while I stayed behind with the students.

Within seconds, the students began saying things like, "I don't know where he's coming from!" and "That's just not true!" One of the students even talked about teachers who did not care as much about her because of her disability. The students were also saying that they knew when teachers were not using equity and gave me specific cases when it was not happening in some of our best schools. The one thing these students agreed on was that all children deserved equity. They vowed to use their voice as student leaders to "demand" it. They clearly supported the work.

While I understood the fact these students waited until after the board members had left as a sign of respect, I was disappointed the board didn't hear the passion in their voices. I appreciated the fact they felt comfortable enough with me to share their thoughts on equity and how they knew when it was not occurring. However, I knew I had more work to do to bring awareness to the case for equity. I found it so ironic the students were advocating for equity on their own behalf as well as their classmates. Shouldn't all of us as educators be advocating just as hard, if not harder?

Lessons Learned

- Children know what equity is.
- Children know that it is every student's right.
- Children know when equity is not happening in the classroom and in their school.
- Children want a voice in big issues affecting them, including issues of equity. ●

I've been in thousands upon thousands of classrooms across the United States, and I can attest to the fact that we have extremely intelligent students. I am in awe of what we can learn from them if we empower them to help us help them. As a principal and superintendent, I held unscripted student town hall meetings to offer middle and high school students the opportunity to ask me any question they wanted. I recall one of these meetings when a white female high school student stood and asked me why it was that some of the students in her school received opportunities that she herself did not receive. She gave me three explicit and detailed examples that supported how she felt, including being on the "standard" track, which had become the pathway we used to tell a student they were not "college material." She was articulate, passionate, and devastated. When I went back to my office and shared this story with my leadership team, they automatically assumed that the girl was black and attended another school. However, she was a white student in one of our best schools. This student had recognized that in her school, many of the teachers seemed to favor some students more than others, and this especially bothered her because she was one who did not receive preferential treatment, and she felt it was because her family was poor and from another country.

Hearing her story bothered my leadership team as much as it bothered me because it was a clear reminder that our students know when we are not treating them fairly and not giving them what they need to be successful. They also know who the favorite students are, and they, in many cases, are not afraid to call it out. As Dr. Martin Luther King Jr. so eloquently put it, "Our lives begin to end the day we become silent about things that matter." In a changing society and as we prepare our students to be globally prepared thinkers, we have a moral imperative to set strong examples for them of how to advocate for all people and to stand up for them and their peers. We can get more done addressing their needs when we allow their voices to guide our work.

LEADING FOR EQUITY NUGGETS

1. Treat each person, regardless of who they are, with respect and fairness. This includes employees, parents, and especially students. As a leader, all of your actions are watched.

2. Build an awareness of the importance of equity in your school community. Many people are not aware of the changing demographics of schools, and as leaders, if we've not shared our specific data with our staff and community, we're doing our organization a disservice. This is not to develop sympathy but rather empathy.

3. Invest time and effort into ongoing, quality cultural competence training that reaches beyond issues of race and allows educators to determine and examine our personal values and biases we exhibit when interacting with children and adults.

4. Take the necessary time to determine what your employees need to address equity from their vantage point. As equity is hard work, including tough conversations surrounding race and poverty, it is important that employees feel supported and are supported to ensure they're successful at their work.

5. Create a risk-free culture that allows folks to make mistakes when addressing equity. With our desire to be politically correct in every area, we must allow our employees to feel free to develop appropriate relationships with students that ultimately lead to specific actions when addressing equity for each student.

6. Review academic outcomes to determine equity disparities: by race, gender, socioeconomic level, disability status, and language proficiency.

7. Involve multiple stakeholders in the conversation as you address equity to ensure everyone understands the academic achievement gaps being targeted.

8. Ask this honest question: What policies do we have in place that further exacerbate achievement gaps or that marginalize certain students?

9. Address equity resource issues head-on: budget allocations, teacher quality, access to technology and other learning resources, supplemental programs and tools, what

(Continued)

(Continued)

students eat for breakfast and lunch in school. I would dare to say that 95 percent of the critical decisions in an organization are those that we, as leaders, are responsible for making. Always keep in mind that our students are watching, so they know when we are not focusing on equity and what really matters, and they are not afraid to call us out on it. Raise your level of expectation for every child to the same level you have for your own families. This raises the bar because we always want to ensure our own family members receive the best resources available. This includes sharing personal stories with our staff about our own families so we connect our values to our leadership.

Additional Resources

Blankstein, A. M., Noguera, P., Kelly, L., & Tutu, D. (2015). *Excellence through equity: Five principles of courageous leadership to guide achievement for every student.* Thousand Oaks, CA: Corwin.

Lindsey, R. B., Robins, K. N., & Terrell, R. D. (2009). *Cultural proficiency: A manual for school leaders* (3rd ed.). Thousand Oaks, CA: Corwin.

Singleton, G. E., & Linton, C. (2006). *Courageous conversations about race: A field guide for achieving equity in schools.* Thousand Oaks, CA: Corwin.

LEADING THE CHANGE

IMPLEMENTING SUCCESSFUL INITIATIVES

If you do not change direction, you may end up where you are heading.

—Lao Tzu

To implement change successfully, leaders need to work with and through people. For this reason alone, people should be important to you. To obtain buy-in for your proposed changes, there are five key steps you should take before you even begin to formulate which changes you would like to implement. If you follow the steps outlined in this chapter, it is much more likely that your initiatives will be successful and that your staff will not only support the decision but also put in the work necessary to make sure that the initiative meets its stated goals. Each of these steps involves working with, working through, and working to understand people.

● ● ● ● TIPS FOR LEADERS ON INITIATING CHANGE

1. Understand the organization's history.
2. Acknowledge the current state of the organization.
3. Understand the "players" within the organization.
4. Teach people to think more broadly about change and what it involves.
5. Develop a deliberate and specific strategy for implementation.

Understand the History of the Organization

People must know that you care about an institution's history. The efforts that you undertake to dig into the background, the efforts of the past leaders, the past successes and failures, and any of the other elements that have worked to advance the organization's mission will be well respected among all you will need as your cohorts.

Taking the time to hear firsthand accounts of the organization's historical past and what veteran staff and community members perceive to be the successes, failures, assets, and shortcomings of the organization will send a clear message to them that you respect them and their contributions. It will also relay a distinct message that you value them; as a result, they are more likely to see you as a leader they should support rather than as a foe to oppose when you attempt to move the organization forward.

Remember, however, that talking to people cannot be an empty exercise created just for show. Value it! What you learn will be of great worth as you put together your strategy for how to produce positive, lasting change—change that lasts beyond you.

●●● THE PRINCIPLE IN ACTION

Listening Must Come First

I was a twenty-four-year-old principal when I took over a school where the previous administrator had served for eight years, and I soon realized that the school was in unequivocal need of change. The demographics of the surrounding community and the school were becoming more and more diverse, and the declining student achievement scores were affecting the school's state accreditation status. The first thing I did was to try to understand the fundamental reason for the decline in student performance. While the quantitative data told one part of the story, I had to do some work to uncover the history of the school and thereby the underlying causes of the decline. This would include lots of conversations with people familiar with the school. I spent hours talking with former principals and teachers, current teachers and staff, and with neighbors around the school—many of whom had lived in the community their entire lives. I also reviewed old yearbooks and used them to reach out to additional people.

My efforts produced these dividends:

1. It gave me the opportunity to learn important information about the school and community's history, which explained important shifts affecting student achievement.

2. It showed the school community that I valued the school's history, a history that they had played a major part in building since the school's establishment 50 years ago.

(Continued)

(Continued)

3. It gained support for me with the school community because my actions showed I valued them by asking for their input. This also made people feel appreciated as valuable contributors to the school's future.

4. It signaled that I was a collaborative leader. Rather than jumping in recklessly, I took time to learn and collect information that would help me draft a strategic approach toward ensuring the school had the solid reputation everyone wanted. These efforts served me well. Not only did they establish me as a deliberate, thorough, and credible leader in the community but learning the school's history also empowered me with the information I needed to create a plan that would ultimately be successful and sustainable over time.

Lessons Learned

- Numbers don't always tell the complete story. Get the data from both sides: qualitative and quantitative.

- We learn best when we listen more than we speak.

- People are more willing to support leadership when they feel the leadership cares about the organization's history. ●

There is more to producing change than charging in and demanding alterations of the present landscape. Ambitious and sometimes overzealous leaders often make this mistake and in doing so permanently compromise their ability to produce and sustain lasting and effective change. Very few leaders last long enough to see any positive changes occur or be sustained. I caution leaders to take some time to understand the history of prior school and district work and initiatives before they begin implementing any changes.

Regardless of where you are tapped to lead, you must recognize that there is a rich, institutional history that preceded you. Having knowledge and awareness of this history is essential to your effectiveness, especially in your efforts to transform the organization and build legacy, which all leaders strive to do. It could very well be that the school has successful initiatives already in place, but as the leader is new, he or she needs to take the time to figure it out. As Irish philosopher and author Edmund Burke stated, "Those who don't know history are doomed to repeat it."

Acknowledge the Current State of the Organization

Before people will allow you to lead them, they want to know you are truly informed about the current state of affairs and that you are not coming into the organization like a tornado making random changes without any regard for its present status. Before they will allow you to show them a new perspective, they must first trust you. Nothing engenders their trust more than your being clear that you are coming from a place of care and operating with an informed strategy—one that is informed by careful research of the past and its players.

If you go into an environment focused simply on your change agenda and are determined to *make* the people fall in line, your efforts will surely fail. I've seen this happen repeatedly. However, if you acknowledge the players, the state of the organization, and

> "If you go into an environment focused simply on your change agenda and are determined to *make* the people fall in line, your efforts will surely fail."

> "However, if you acknowledge the players, the state of the organization, and the past processes that resulted in the current situation you now face, the people, confident that you understand them and their reality, will be more inclined to allow you to lead them forward."

the past processes that resulted in the current situation you now face, the people, confident that you understand them and their reality, will be more inclined to allow you to lead them forward.

●●● THE PRINCIPLE IN ACTION

She Was Right

As a new principal, I was burrowing into the historical background of the school when I had a conversation with Brenda, the seventh-grade English teacher. The conversation started something like this:

Brenda: You will be my fourth principal. I was here before you got here, I'm here now, and I will still be here when you leave.

Me: You probably will be.

We laughed and then embraced.

Rather than feel challenged by a teacher with such a strong position, I appreciated her candor. I recognized what a valuable resource she would be in helping me to understand my new landscape. It did not take long for Brenda's value to become crystal clear. She allowed me to pick her brain, and because of her rich past with the school and her experience in having witnessed the various leadership transitions, she could help me think through things in a way that few others could have. If I needed to understand why something existed as it did or why certain people were on board and others were not, all I had to do was ask Brenda. She was a walking, talking historical record ready to spill the secrets and inner workings of the past with only a moment's request. Brenda was vital to my success as a principal. Furthermore, in the end, Brenda proved to be right, just like she'd said: she stayed at the school long after me!

Lessons Learned

- As a leader, never be afraid of strong personalities. Leadership is not about a title or a position.

- As a leader, we must make sure that we are always willing to learn. Modeling this type of behavior sets a tone for the organization that everyone should be learning and growing. ●

People want leadership! However, you are initially an outsider, and they will probably be thinking, *We've seen this before! This person is just coming in here making impromptu changes, so we know that the modifications are not going to work!* Having such an outlook produces a general attitude of distrust for the new leader, and distrust in an environment makes it awfully hard for a leader to implement change. As a matter of fact, it makes it next to impossible to do anything!

For best results when learning about the organization prior to change, focus as much as possible on what the organization's culture looks and feels like—how business is really done. Your ability to unite the people around your goal depends on it. This is something again that my late grandmother often emphasized to me.

They Told Me to Do It NOW!

A colleague of mine accepted a superintendent position. He asked me to be his mentor, and I agreed. In a conversation I had with him just prior to his beginning the job, he proceeded to tell me all the things he thought were wrong with the school district. I listened for a good fifteen minutes, and then I asked him a simple question:

Me: What are you going to do about it?

Him: Change it!

Me: How?

Him: I'm just going to change it!

I continued with asking him if he understood the history, the players, the context, and the other factors at work that had led to the current condition of the district. He replied by explaining that the school board had basically said to him, "You're the superintendent, so change it!" Thus, he planned to just go in and change things—*now!*

To make a long story short, within two months, I was recommending an employment attorney to negotiate this individual's exit package. You see, even though the school board gave him the title and power to make alterations, they soon backed away from him because they were receiving too many negative responses from the community.

Lessons Learned

- Even though we hold the power to demand change, this does not mean that we have the authority to implement or even attempt change. There should always be a well-developed strategy underlying sustainable change efforts, and this should essentially include the input and support of the people who will be most affected by the change. In a manner of speaking, people must give you the authority to implement successful and sustainable change. If an organization changes just because you say so, it will change back as soon as you leave. Dictated change will only last while the dictator is in place. The changes will not be sustained. I know we have all seen this.

- Every boss gives his or her employee a charge to get "it" done. However, the charge does not come at the sacrifice of the strategy. When times get tough, the strategy will become more important than the reason behind why the charge was given. ●

Take the time to understand and then publicly acknowledge your intimate awareness with the current state of the organization. Explain the research that you have done, the records that you have reviewed, and the people with whom you have spoken. Make a concerted effort to convince people of your fastidiousness and that you have developed a customized, well-informed, carefully constructed, and intelligent strategy for managing change based upon the unique state of the organization. This will eliminate fear because when you position your approach in such a way, you're using honey, and we all know this old phrase: you get more flies with honey than vinegar.

Understand the "Players" Within the Organization

Every individual in an organization is important. Everyone has value. I get it. However, as a change leader, I also understand that there are some people who emerge as more influential, particularly when it comes to moving an agenda forward and managing change. Thus, as soon as you are selected to lead an organization, you must ask two questions:

1. Who in this organization will be most instrumental in helping me get things done and manage change?
2. Who is most influential in helping me to move the organization forward?

Every organization has its team of players or key influencers, both internally and externally, so look for them. These are individuals who have a voice with other people, and they possess a level of power and authority, de jure or de facto, that can easily sway the opinion of others. What they tell people to do, in most cases, people will do—good or bad. Whatever position they tell people to take, in many cases, people will take—positive or negative. Something about the way that these individuals operate has made them leaders, so like it or not, they possess the voice, power, and level of influence over people that you do not possess initially. They were there when you came on the scene, and most likely, they will be there when you make your departure. Hence, Exhibit A: people such as Brenda. Thus, if you are to be an effective leader, you must learn how to work with these influential people to get the work done.

You have two choices of how to approach these key influencers:

1. Disparage the power they possess because it is initially more potent than your own.
2. Use these critical players to your advantage.

As an effective leader, I have always done the latter, and this decision has always proven to be immensely successful.

We Were a True Team

When I became a principal, I was fortunate enough to have a key asset on my side: Lynette, the school's assistant principal. She was a staple at the school and one of the first people I met when I started. Lynette had been an assistant principal at the school for many years, and although she was exceptional in her role, she never had a desire to be a principal. I saw that she loved the school, and I recognized immediately her value to the organization. Most of all, I realized that I needed her, so I was intent on building a very strong relationship with her, which still exists.

After talking with Lynette, it was clear that she understood what needed to be saved and what needed to be changed. We had many long conversations, and together, we worked to develop a change strategy. Of course, a major part of this strategy was to get out into the community and build awareness of what the data were saying and how certain factors were affecting our students. For example, a new middle school had just opened in our school system and split our students; the more affluent students in the community, as well as some of our best teachers, went to the new school. Thus, it was important for us to help the people in the community understand that the school they were now seeing was not the same one they had known before the new school opened. As a result, it would be necessary for us to change several things: our approach to teaching, our approach to our relationships with our students, and even our approach to how we engaged our parents. The school had been accustomed to parents' attending PTA meetings, being actively involved in the life of the school, and supporting the students financially. However, the bulk of those involved parents left a void when their children transferred to the

(Continued)

(Continued)

new building. We, too, were essentially a new school and a new school community.

We realized that we had to implement a comprehensive change strategy to adjust to our new normal. As the principal, I knew I could not do it alone; there was too much history here. I knew that Lynette needed to be on board because of her history and her relationship. People knew her and trusted her. Thus, I relied on Lynette to assist me in advancing our work. Together, we pitched the strategy and talked about it to everyone as a duo. Lynette trusted me, and I trusted her. We did great things for our school and the surrounding community, including implementing a strategic plan, regaining our accreditation status, and building a sense of school pride among teachers, students, and community. This became evident with the introduction of Cubbie, our school's mascot, who I dressed up as one day for our students.

Lesson Learned

- You never had to do it all yourself, and you should not attempt to do so. Understanding who the players are will assist you in determining who should drive which part of the work. With the right team, as Muhammad Ali said, "Impossible is nothing." •

When introducing change, you need to be the key messenger, but you should not be the *only* messenger! Recruit those within the organization who can have an impact on and influence others in ways you cannot.

> "When introducing change . . . recruit those within the organization who can have an impact on and influence others in ways you cannot."

Typically, the voices of three to five players stand out in an organization. The number may vary based on its size. As a leader, one of the first items on your agenda must be to get to know who these key players are. Fortunately, through experience, I have mastered the process of discovering and connecting with these influential individuals. I follow a three-step process.

1. Talk to about five random people in the organization and ask this question: Who do I need to get to know?

Within the first week of my appointment as superintendent, I met with all twelve board members and asked them whom they felt I needed to meet. They provided me with a list of people they felt were important, and I entertained all their local, state, and national recommendations.

2. List all the names people give you. One or two names will usually appear repeatedly. These are the key influencers, those whom people deem to be their "real" leaders. They are not higher-ups with an agenda; they are peers, individuals who operate on the same level, and this alone gives them a level of trustworthiness that is difficult for the leader to gain. Remember to ask, recruit, and seek internal as well as external folks.

When my board members gave me the suggested names, five names continuously came up. I immediately reached out to each of these five key influencers. The list consisted of a union leader, an elected official, a former teacher, and two parents. During my entire tenure as a superintendent, I made it a point to speak with each of them at least once monthly. They sustained me on several tough key issues.

3. Meet as early as possible with the key influencers. Whether they influence people in a positive or negative direction, they have a powerful level of sway, so you must connect early and often with them. If you do not connect with them at the beginning, it could mean potential doom for any of your future work. If they do not like any part of your plans, they will ensure that others do not like it either. The result will be this: You will find yourself fighting an uphill battle—one that you could have avoided. Always remember that there's only one of you and many of them! You begin as the outsider.

I met with each of the five key influencers whom my board members suggested. Then, during each of the influencers' meetings, I asked them whom they thought I needed to meet. Again, I took note of the names that repeatedly emerged, and I made an additional list of new names. When names start to repeat themselves, you can be sure that you probably have covered the range of influencers. I followed up on each of these individuals with a contact, a meeting, and coffee and made sure I was flexible to meet at all times of the day. As a result, each of these individuals became a key player in my strategy, moving our work forward and helping to ensure our success. Relationships matter.

When you meet with the key influencers, you stand a fifty-fifty chance of them being for you or against you, but the odds are more in your favor. Giving them a bit of your time is important. People like time with the leader. Build a relationship with them *quickly* and always nurture it. Then, bring them into the conversation about the possible need for change, and ask for their input on how to execute the plan.

Explain the approach you believe the organization should take, and recruit their voices and power as an extension of your own to build support. Lastly, always remember to get their advice.

Explaining the need for change is essential and is a critical step in getting people engaged in the change process. As you are building your case for why change is necessary, reflect on these questions:

● ● ● ● BUILDING THE CASE FOR CHANGE

- What data can I present to best articulate our reality?
- What stories can I tell to put our reality in context?
- What examples can I use to get others to understand the big picture?
- What other compelling evidence can I introduce to present the case?

Be intentional about building your case. Most people grow frustrated with change because they feel it's being introduced for the sake of it. However, if you take the time to build a compelling case for why change is necessary and the benefits it will bring first to students and then to them, you increase the chances they will join your team and your efforts. In fact, even when you have to implement change that might not be popular, if the case has been made for why, the likelihood of success still is higher than the case not being made.

Reducing Class Sizes

A big issue confronting me when I became a superintendent was large class sizes in our high schools. A reporter from the local newspaper compiled a database of information by school so parents could search easily and realize the overcrowding of their children's classrooms. I had to address the issue. I talked to dozens of teachers and leaders who all agreed that large class sizes were unacceptable. The *why* seemed to be easy in this case, but I knew we still had to develop a strategy for implementing the *how*.

It was clear to the teachers, to the leaders, and to me that we had to look at the two factors behind large class sizes: teacher allocations and school schedules. After working with a third-party consultant and a district steering committee, the changes we proposed focused on school scheduling. In several cases, high schools were on different schedules. Some students took six classes, some took seven classes, and some took eight classes. For more even teacher distribution, we had to implement a countywide schedule with all students taking eight classes over the course of the school year. However, because there were twenty-four high schools, it should come as no surprise there were several resisters. One school's staff members did not want any part of the change. I fielded many complaints from people, including elected officials, who pressed me to leave the school alone since its firmly ingrained schedule was two decades old. A seemingly popular elected official even told me the school was "untouchable!"

This type of school and its community required a different approach. I intentionally focused on how to support the school's staff and parents throughout the entire change process. I assured them that I would give them whatever they needed for a successful transition, which included phasing out their current schedule and allowing flexibility for students in upper grades. In the end, the school changed its class sizes like the rest of the other high schools in the district. Not everyone was happy, but the initiative was nonetheless successful.

Lessons Learned

- Even in the best circumstances, note everyone will agree that change should occur. However, with a strong case for why, the likelihood of success is greater than if no case is made.

- When possible, flexibility with the timing for implementation can ease anxiety. The community will take note of your willingness to be flexible. ●

When people seem initially against you, don't let it deter you; people often resist what they do not know. Details are always sketchiest at the beginning of any initiative, so rather than feeling dejected and discouraged by opposition, say to yourself, "I've got to do a better job in detailing and communicating my plan!" Collaborative, reflective leaders also try to look for ways to incorporate ideas from stakeholders who will be most affected by the change. Frankly, some of the best change results from leaders creating a framework for change and building the internal workings of the model with the team. This is a more empowering posture to take as a leader, and besides, it's the best way to ensure sustainability of the change.

Again, I should warn you that in dealing with change and change management, not everyone is going to come on board. There are individuals who always ask the same question: When should I move forward? The answer is this: it depends. Ask yourself these four questions:

● ● ● ● POINTS TO CONSIDER BEFORE PROPOSING A CHANGE

1. Have I clearly analyzed available quantitative and qualitative data to make the case for *why*?

2. Have I done a thorough analysis to determine the best course of action needed to ensure implementation to achieve the desired goal, including involving others impacted by the change?

3. What are the critical supports needed to ensure my employees can absorb, adjust to, and implement the change?

4. Do I have a sound strategy for how I will communicate the change internally and externally?

Don't be naive in believing everyone will support you, but if you can answer these four essential questions in the affirmative, the chances of a successful implementation of the change will be greater with appropriate monitoring.

After you propose the change strategy, step back and give your people time; you owe them that. Again, I am reasonably impatient and usually think that giving people this extra time for contemplation can seem like a waste, but I have learned over the years that they deserve time to process the change. Never forget that organizations are about people, and they matter! Research on temperaments suggests that the ability to accept change and to embrace change is easier for some personality types than others. Most worry about what will be required to support change and how the change will affect them personally. Thus, after you have spoken with those who oppose the change, listened to their point of view and received their input and suggestions, and helped them to understand the why, give them some space to process. Remember, you need other messengers doing the same thing. They need an opportunity to process how the changes will affect their work, time, and resources as well as the overall effect that it will have on their lives, both directly and indirectly. They need to know you will support them.

●●● THE PRINCIPLE IN ACTION

Is Now the Right Time?

When I was a district administrator, our school system had a policy that required younger students who lived one mile or less away from their school to walk to school. Those who lived more than a mile away traveled by bus to school. The same policy applied to high school students, but the distance was two miles. We discovered, however, that we had been busing students from a subdivision that was located less than one mile away from the school. To comply with policy, we could have easily made the decision and said, "This is the district policy, and the students from this subdivision will immediately begin walking to school!" However, I resisted enacting such drastic change simply because of policy. Students had been bused from this subdivision for over five years, and an abrupt change would have surely disrupted the lives of the students and their families and caused a community uproar. Instead, I delayed the busing until the next school year, giving families several notices to give them ample time to adapt.

Lesson Learned

- With change, timing matters. Just because you have the power and ability to make immediate change does not mean that you must immediately do so. Consider your timing and the time that it will take others to absorb the change because it will have a significant impact on a change being successfully implemented or causing it to fail. Gradual change in most cases leads to sustainable change. ●

If my experience is any indication, resistant colleagues or community members will eventually acquiesce—even if only for more conversation or for a greater understanding of the proposal. This willingness to engage in further dialogue could be a result of having a greater level of acceptance after they had scrutinized the change, after they had an opportunity to voice input, after they had realized that the change was inevitable, or after they had seen that those they influenced realized the value of the proposed change. Whatever the reason, take advantage of their willingness to listen so that you can continue the dialogue and encourage them to be a component of the change strategy. Give them a prominent role that will make them feel valuable. After all, it's difficult to bash something that you had a hand in creating! When you have the support of these individuals, you will ultimately gain most of the support of everyone under their influence. When others try to criticize you, you need players like this who are on your side who will step up and support you.

> " . . . Continue the dialogue and encourage them to be a component of the change strategy. Give them a prominent role that will make them feel valuable. After all, it's difficult to bash something that you had a hand in creating!"

●●● THE PRINCIPLE IN ACTION

Find an Insider Advocate

While I was working as a district administrator in Houston, one of the schools in my district was failing. The school was constantly losing its students to charter schools because parents did not want to send their children to a school with such a poor reputation. However, the community in which the school was located was a vocal community that fought change. Despite the years of low student performance and many members of the community recognizing the need to do something different, which they vocalized several times including in the media, the community did not want us to close the school, which was the originally recommendation prior to my arrival. The community continued to fight to keep it open because it symbolized to them a community tradition since it was the first African-American junior high school in Houston.

I knew that the school needed to improve, but as an outsider, I knew that the main drive for change had to come from the community members themselves. Before change could occur, the community needed to articulate in their own words that the performance of the school was unacceptable. I wanted the parents to collectively pledge to put pressure on me. Furthermore, as the school was in a predominantly African-American neighborhood with a long and proud history, I had an idea of turning the school into an academy exclusively for African-American boys. I had done research on the idea by looking at a similar model in Chicago, and I had introduced the idea to several elected officials in Houston. Although we thought that making the change was a good idea, we felt that since this community historically resisted change, they would sense that they were losing something, particularly with the changing of the school's name, even though they recognized the school's performance was among the lowest in the school system.

To win support for the African-American boys academy, I held a community meeting with a panel that included students, parents, teachers, elected officials, and community influencers to talk about improving the achievement of African-American males. However, I also strategically planted someone in the audience to say, "This community should work together to build a boys school so that our sons will receive a first rate education." When they heard one of their

(Continued)

(Continued)

own introduce this suggestion, the people entertained it and discussed it, and after several weeks of thinking about the proposal, they enthusiastically embraced it. They thought it was a great idea!

From there, I worked with the people in the entire community to transform the failing coed school to an all-male prep academy for Grades 6 through 12. This school is now an amazing success and is graduating young men of all backgrounds who are attending some of the top colleges and universities across the country.

Lesson Learned

- If you don't have a relationship with the group to whom you are trying to introduce change, use an insider to advocate for your change rather than doing it yourself. People do not look kindly on outsiders coming in and trying to push change on them. You might not get the credit for introducing the idea, but who cares? If the change happens, everyone wins, and helping people and organizations win is what leadership is all about. President Harry Truman once said, "It is amazing what you can accomplish if you do not care who gets the credit." •

One thing I have observed over the years among some of the leaders with whom I've worked is that although they desire to be effective, oftentimes many are not willing to go beyond this desire to invest the time and strategy that are necessary to be effective. Leadership is strategy. I coach leaders on how to develop an effective strategy based on whatever goals they want to accomplish. I ask the right questions to match the appropriate strategy. Not everything that worked for me may work for you, but with the definitive questions, a sound strategy can be cultivated and applied. Developing a winning strategy around change takes time. Don't rush. Don't cut corners.

Accomplished leaders will unanimously attest to the fact that effectiveness requires a time commitment to engage people on this level. I am committed to doing what is needed to be effective, regardless of how long it takes; therefore, I often find myself stifling my impatience in the short term so more students reap the benefits in the long term.

Some may object and say, "Isn't this just politics? I don't have time for politics." My response is this: If you don't have time for politics, you do not have time to be an effective leader. Politics is here to stay. Change management requires the leadership of people. You don't have to play politics—and you shouldn't—but you *do* have to know politics. Know the right people, and use the right strategy to accomplish your goals.

Ensure People Understand What Change Means

Some people are resistant to change because they hold preconceived notions about how change will look, how it will radically disturb the status quo, and how severe of an impact it will have on their world and on the world around them. They think of change in terms of extremes, as something drastic. If you are to be effective in managing change, it will be your job as a leader not only to lead change but to lead people in thinking more broadly about the concept of change itself.

Your goal in shaping people's readiness for change will be to reorient their thinking by proposing two questions:

1. *What does this organization need to be successful?*
2. *What do our students need to be successful?*

Have them consider the questions carefully, and when they respond, pull their ideas into the mix. If you can subtlety convince them about the need for change based on the desire for the organization and the students to be successful, everyone wins!

Defining change in an organization need not be a complex task. Change—either large or small—merely represents anything different from what the organization is currently experiencing, and the magnitude is relative to an individual's perception.

Approach any modifications in a management strategy cautiously. The changes we often consider to be of little consequence can magnify into a near disaster. For example, you might feel the need to cancel the school's annual winter concert. You assume this variance will have no repercussions only to find yourself in a firestorm of community complaints because the twenty-year concert is a sacred cow.

●●● THE PRINCIPLE IN ACTION

The Math Problem

I can recall one instance in which a change I implemented did not go well. As the assistant principal, I was responsible for the school's master schedule, and after reviewing our math data, I wanted to ensure our ninth-grade students who were taking Algebra I were set up for success. The data clearly indicated the need for our best math teachers to instruct those thirty-five percent of our freshmen who did not take Algebra I prior to high school. In further reviewing data, I found that we had four solid math teachers with strong scores, so in developing the master schedule and assigning teachers, I made sure three of those teachers had the Algebra I classes and a common planning time each day. Although my decision, based on data, seemed perfectly justified, I failed to consider the need to communicate with these three math teachers. When they discovered the new schedule, two of the math teachers resigned from our school before the new school year began because, according to them, I failed to interact with them before making the schedule modifications.

Lesson Learned

- You must have a strategic plan in place for how to make change, and you must communicate with all whom the change will affect. I should have involved the math department chair and these teachers before designating their new assignments, and I should have explained why our neediest students required our best teachers. Although they might not have readily embraced the change, they would have had the opportunity for rebuttal. Had I explained how a daily in-common planning period and complete backing from the administration would offer them solid support, two of my best math teachers might have remained in our building. How I wished I had approached that change differently! ●

Change to you might seem as simple as changing the name of the Christmas concert to winter concert because of the growing diversity of the school's population. In fact, a principal colleague of mine attempted to make this change, and the reaction from her school community was *massive*! She had no idea that her community would interpret a "simple" modification as a *colossal* change! In any case, she made the change, and it represented something different from previous years at the school. She learned that she needed to build the case strategically, delicately, and effectively. Changing the concert's name was not the issue but rather how she went about it and communicated it (or failed to do so).

A Change for Student Safety

I had a principal contact me about a change situation that he was encountering. He wanted to modify the pickup and drop-off location at the school because it would increase student safety. (To him) this did not seem like a complex change issue that required a well-developed strategy. It would simply involve making a declaration that the pickup and drop-off location was moving from Point A to Point B and using signage to route the parents over to the new spot. He saw it as a trivial change, at best. He was less than twenty-four hours into the change when he called me. I asked him several tough questions, including why he wanted to change the location. Was the timing right for the change? Were there others who also saw the need and voiced the need for the change? Did he have any data on potential student safety issues due to the location? Where was his parent-teacher association regarding the change? With all questions, he realized he had missed a few important steps.

While he viewed this as a simple change, was he *ever* wrong! Parents were in an uproar, the teachers were upset, and everyone rallied against him. He was astonished and felt like he was the only one who saw this need to improve student safety. Putting out the fires that this "simple" change caused in his school took a great of his time, and as a result, the commotion diverted his focus and attention from the other more critical school issues.

Lesson Learned

- Regardless of how major or minor you perceive a change to be, it will require a careful change strategy to be effective, including getting buy-in with individuals who will be most impacted by the change. In this case, that group was parents who felt left out of the conversation. ●

Have an Effective Strategy to Implement Change

No good leader approaches a change process randomly. While it might be tempting to enter an organization, observe what you perceive needs to be changed, and dive right in, such an unsystematic and haphazard approach will likely produce sporadic, low-quality, and unsustainable results. What's worse, you are very likely to leave in your wake a trail of unhappy, offended, and resentful people who might feel compelled to sabotage your future efforts rather than support them.

Instead, all change processes must proceed consistently with a carefully planned strategy that will include the input of those affected. Your change mantra should not be "Team Me"; it should be "Team We." Why? It's simple; *you* cannot produce sustainable change that is, most importantly, accepted, maintained, and supported by those in the organization without the participation of those people.

●●● THE PRINCIPLE IN ACTION

Going Digital

While I was a superintendent, our system implemented a major instructional initiative for the classroom, a move meant to close the digital divide by assigning all our students their own computers. We began the implementation by distributing computers to our teachers and redesigning the curriculum, the resources, and the professional development. We then led the distribution with our elementary

(Continued)

(Continued)

school students, followed by our middle school students, and finally concluded the process with our high school students. This was a massive change in our district and was the largest one-to-one initiative in the nation for the distribution of technology in all grades. Thus, we had to engage in some strategic planning and implementation.

We decided to begin the process of implementation as soon as I arrived; however, by "begin," I do not mean distributing computers. Instead, we began planning—a critical part of the change implementation process. Before we ever distributed a single computer to our teachers or students, we chose to utilize eighteen months solely for planning and for talking to people—students, parents, teachers, administrators, and elected officials who funded us—about the proposed change and what it meant across the organization. Because we invested quality time in planning, the challenges were controllable. While a handful of critics voiced their opinions, the program received sweeping support from both our schools and our community.

Lessons Learned

- In order for any change to be successful, planning has to come first. Strategically plan for all *what if* scenarios—especially what different types of support employees will need. Whatever you do, do not rush the planning process.

- Never underestimate the value of communication when implementing change. The more information people know and hear directly from the leadership, the less likely they will be to rely on other, perhaps fabricated, information. ●

When people reject a potentially positive change, it could be because of the way it is proposed. Thus, leaders must thoughtfully consider how to introduce change. Leaders are often accused of having a "ready, fire!" mentality; they propose what they think is a good idea, and they immediately set the wheels in motion to implement the change. From their point of view, because the conditions necessitating the change are often so critical, there is no time to waste. However, without the proper planning, the changes they attempt to implement often encounter resistance within the organization. The change can go unsupported and possibly sabotaged. In the "ready, aim, fire!" approach, the "aim" should be planning— and there should be *lots of it*.

You *must* include people in the development of the change strategy to give them a sense of ownership and foster a sense of acknowledgment to whatever change strategy you ultimately develop. Two of my mentors, the late Dr. William C. Bosher, who was the former state superintendent for Virginia, cochair of my superintendent transition team, and my dissertation chair, and Dr. William Hite, who was my first principal, always stressed the importance of learning as much as I could from people, and that can only be achieved by listening more than speaking. Regardless of an individual's title, he or she can teach you something. Therefore, listen to the stories of people, invite their ideas and suggestions, and implement them into the change strategy. Why work alone and potentially face resistance when you can enlist the help of others?

In some instances, a new leader will encounter challenges that can be easily modified. When you recognize these opportunities arise, seize them! Go for these quick wins by putting together a change strategy that you can effortlessly execute over a short time. Racking up a series of these small wins will not only help to establish your reputation as a new leader who gets things done—building capital—but it will also boost your confidence. Consequently, you can stash away your energy for the changes that will require more detailed, collaborative planning and strategizing.

Before approaching changes, a leader must select those that will reap the most benefits. Start first with the issues of highest priority, and then work your way down the list and address the areas that seem marginal. Remember, timing is important, and everything is not important at the present moment. New leaders always struggle with prioritizing, but the solution is to use qualitative and quantitative data centered on safety, student achievement, communications, and organizational effectiveness. These four areas allow us to determine what crucial needs demand initial attention, and asking your staff three essential questions can solve this.

A GUIDE TO PRIORITIZING INITIATIVES

1. Select initiatives that will reap the most benefits.

2. Use qualitative and quantitative data to help determine priority of initiatives.

3. Data should focus on safety, student achievement, communications, and organizational effectiveness.

4. Ask your team these questions:
   o What are the successes of this organization?
   o How does this organization and its actions need to be improved?
   o If you were me, what would be your focus to ensure our organization's success?

---

5. Based on the data you have collected, choose two or three top issues to tackle first; rank other necessary changes in descending order.

6. Other questions to consider are these:

   o Do we need to make this change at all?

   o Do we need to make this change now?

   o Whom will the change affect the most?

   o How will this change affect the people, the school climate, or the organizational culture?

   o Will the implemented change have a profound negative affect on the day-to-day life of your team members?

   o How will the change affect the most vulnerable of your community?

   o Is your planned change strategy effective? Does it take into account the needs of the individuals in your community?

You must resist changing every issue immediately. When everything is a priority, nothing is a priority. Thus, choose two or three top items to tackle initially, rank all the other needed changes in descending order, and then address them in sequence.

For example, you might be a district leader who wants to change the pay schedule of your employees because you realize that you can save the district a great deal of money by doing payroll once a month as opposed to twice a month. However, before you begin trying to implement such a change, there are things to consider:

• How long has the district been operating on a two-paycheck-per-month schedule?

- Why does the district pay its employees twice a month as opposed to once a month?
- Has it ever been a once-a-month payment system?
- Who will be the most vocal if you change the pay schedule?

If you are picking a battle that is going to upset 90 percent of the people in your district, you might need to reconsider introducing such a change, regardless of the savings.

As noted earlier, when you are weighing the pros and cons of introducing change, it's always most important to question its timing. For example, for each item on your list of changes, you should ask yourself questions like these: Do we need to make this change *at all*? Do we need to make this change *right now*? Consider also what people will feel is the strongest impact from the change. How will the change affect the people, the school climate, or the organizational culture? Will the cafeteria workers or the custodians, who count on receiving two checks per month, be able to survive such a big shift in their pay schedule? Is the impact that the change will have on these key individuals worth the few hundreds of thousands of dollars that the district may save? Is it really all about the budget savings, or should consideration for people's lives be as monumental as the money you stand to save? These considerations are worthy of review before you choose to implement any change.

I cannot emphasize strongly enough that change is about people. Thus, if your change strategy will be effective, your ability to work with people must be equally effective. The development of a good change strategy always begins with the new leader's polling the people who it will affect the most. When you listen closely, you will begin to see trends emerge among the people's answers. Excavating this valuable information will help you to develop a change strategy that is sure to succeed.

LEADING CHANGE NUGGETS

1. Have knowledge and awareness of the organization's history to enhance the legacy before making any changes. The organization's history means talking to people who were there before you arrived.

2. Analyze the current state of affairs within the organization to determine the best way forward. The organization's current state of affairs means focusing as much as possible on the organization's culture. Take the time to understand and then publicly acknowledge your personal interest. To build credibility, explain the research you have done, the records you have reviewed, and the people with whom you have spoken.

3. Determine the key players in an organization, and build relationships with them quickly. The organization has its team of players, or key influencers, internally and externally—look for them. When introducing change, you need to be the *key* messenger, but you do not necessarily need to be the *only* messenger! Allow those key influencers to be your spokespersons.

4. Ensure people within the organization understand what change means for the organization and for them. The organization looks to its leader as the professional developer who will help develop necessary modifications. To shape an organization's change readiness, the leader must encourage the members to think about and to answer this question: What does our organization need to be

(Continued)

(Continued)

successful? This discussion rallies the members to be a part of the solution.

5. Develop a deliberate and specific strategy for implementation, including a communications plan. All change must proceed according to a carefully planned strategy, and no strategy will be effective unless you are able to get people on board, get their input on the development, and harness their collective efforts to produce sustainable change for the specific goal. Don't rush. When developing the strategy, consider the timing of the change.

Additional Resources

Bridges, W. (2009). *Managing transitions: Making the most of change.* London, England: Nicholas Brealey.

Fullan, M. (2011). *The six secrets of change: What the best leaders do to help their organizations survive and thrive.* San Francisco, CA: Jossey-Bass.

Harvard Business Review. (2011). *HBR's 10 Must Reads on Change Management.* Boston, MA: Harvard Business Review Press.

Heath, C., & Heath, D. (2010). *Switch: How to change things when change is hard.* New York, NY: Broadway Books.

Heifetz, R. A., Grashow, A., & Linsky, M. (2009). *The practice of adaptive leadership: Tools and tactics for changing your organization and the world.* Boston, MA: Harvard Business Press.

Kahan, S. (2010). *Getting change right: How leaders transform organizations from the inside out.* San Francisco, CA: Jossey-Bass.

Kotter, J. P. (2012). *Leading change.* Boston, MA: Harvard Business Review Press.

Wagner, T., Kegan, R., Lahey, L. L., Lemons, R. W., Garnier, J., Helsing, D., & Ark, T. V. (2006). *Change leadership: A practical guide to transforming our schools.* San Francisco, CA: Jossey-Bass.

LEADING THROUGH COMMUNICATION

TELLING YOUR OWN STORY

> *The single biggest problem in communication is the illusion that it has taken place.*
>
> —George Bernard Shaw

I admire great leaders, and John Francis "Jack" Welch, former chair and CEO of General Electric and an organizational leadership expert, often talked about one of the keys to making his company effective: communicate with simplicity, consistency, and repetition. He urged the people within his organization to communicate relentlessly!

People might look at pioneering examples like a Jack Welch and say, "Yeah, but there had to be a *lot* more than communication that made the organization so stellar!" This is a typical response because it is common for people to discount the contribution that communication can make toward the effectiveness of an organization. I happen to agree with Mr. Welch, who, according to Michael Useem, William and Jacalyn Egan Professor of Management and director of the Wharton Center for Leadership and Change Management, is "exceptionally talented at communication." I believe that communication plays a much more compelling role in building an effective organization than people give it credit for. Because they minimize its significance, they do not focus on their own communication efforts; therefore, they do not build effective organizations.

> "Communication plays a much more compelling role in building an effective organization than people give it credit for."

As superintendent, I was honored by the American Association of School Administrators (AASA) with its Leadership Through Communication Award. AASA awards this honor to superintendents who are exceptional in communicating their message to the communities that they serve, and I was humbled to receive such an accolade from my peers. This award further emphasized to me the importance of deliberate communication.

Communication can prove challenging in any organizational context, but it is a necessity for effective leadership. As I plan my schedule each day, I always include communication as a key consideration. When I led a district with over 21,000 employees and more than 112,000 students, I approached my communications strategically. At the start of each day, I would ask myself the following questions:

- With whom do I need to communicate today?
- How will I communicate with these individuals?
- What message(s) will I convey?
- What is the key to effectively communicating with these individuals?

As I thought about these questions, I used them to develop strategies that would help me to effectively convey my thoughts and elicit responses. This type of forethought has served me well throughout my career.

●●● THE PRINCIPLE IN ACTION

The Right Match

If you are a leader in an organization, it is imperative that someone whose communication style matches yours assists you. For example, if you are in the field of education and you are a principal, your secretary will be that key person working with you to communicate to others. If you are a superintendent, your communication liaison will be someone such as a chief communications officer. All organizations need someone alongside the leader to tailor the message.

When I first became a superintendent, I realized that my district's present chief communications officer and I did not have compatible styles, especially when talking to the press. I replaced her with Mychael Dickerson, a master communicator whom I knew from my days as a school principal. I selected him not only because he was smart but because he also reflected qualities and methods that I believed to be necessary in effective communication.

Mychael and I strategically and effectively addressed many issues concerning our schools, our community, and our district. Mychael or one of his team members was always present to develop a communication plan for any issue. Because I had someone who matched my communication style, I heard countless times that our community received more communication and felt more engaged than ever before. In our yearly stakeholder survey, our communication received an 80 percent rating for being open, timely, and transparent.

(Continued)

Lesson Learned

- You must have someone who is compatible with you in assisting with communicating your message. Strategically hiring someone who was dynamic and compatible to fill the role of chief communication officer was by far one of the best decisions I made as a superintendent! ●

Organizational leaders seeking to maximize their communication effectiveness should carefully consider the following seven key tips.

● ● ● ● TIPS FOR LEADERS ON MAXIMIZING COMMUNICATION EFFECTIVENESS

1. Communicate openly, honestly, and in a timely manner.

2. Communicate your story, or someone else will.

3. Organize your communication efforts.

4. Individualize your communication when it really matters.

5. Use every available resource to communicate.

6. View communication as a two-way street.

7. Have an open-door communication policy.

Communicate Openly, Honestly, and in a Timely Manner

I would like to share two things about me and the way I communicate. First, like many people, I don't like surprises—not for birthdays, not for other types of celebrations, and especially not with communications. When it comes to communication, I always operate from the perspective that because I do not like surprises, I don't like to surprise other people. This was especially true with my school board—no surprises.

Secondly, what you see is what you get. Anyone who has worked with me for any amount of time can attest that I am going to tell you the truth. This is especially true for times when I must correct or discuss "touchy" or "sensitive" subjects—subjects around which other people tend to dance instead of approaching them in a transparent and straightforward manner. Over the years, I have developed a skill that allows me to temper truthfulness with a great deal of tact as I share my feelings about an issue. I've learned this through personal experiences, through training sessions, and by observing how role models conduct themselves. Most importantly, whenever I have to address a sensitive subject with someone, I always speak with the utmost respect so that by the end of our talk, the individual knows my remarks were not personal; the individual understands my position and how improvement can occur. It is important to note that people should always feel respected in all situations. We all deserve that.

Leaving people empowered with how to proceed in the future is an especially important element of truthfulness in communication. If you, as the leader, do not provide them with such insights for the future, they are prone to repeat the same actions that brought on the conversation in the first place. Therefore, you owe it to them to explain fully what they *should* do to produce the results you would like to see. Everyone wants clear expectations.

Don't Let Kindness Cloud Clarity

I thoroughly enjoy observing classrooms, and I specifically made time for them in my early days as an administrator. I remember one time when a classroom observation was hugely disappointing. This individual had been teaching for years, so I had to be carefully sensitive with how I conducted the post-observation conference. When the time came for us to discuss the results of her observation, I began by being very complimentary. I tried to talk about the good things that I'd observed since you should always begin by trying to find something that works. Here was the problem: While I was attempting to find something that worked—when, according to my observation, essentially *nothing* had worked at all—I, unfortunately, confused the teacher. At the end of the conference, she did not realize that the observation was not good, and in her words, she was pleased things had gone so well! I later sent this teacher four different messages pertaining to the poor observation, and each time, she misinterpreted my messages. She never recognized that she'd received a bad observation. In the end, I don't know who was more confused—the teacher or me.

The fact that the teacher had walked away each time from our communication without understanding that she needed to make some significant changes in her classroom was my failure. I owned that! I had focused so much on making sure that the discussion was amiable that the fundamental message had been lost.

Lesson Learned

- While it is true that leaders need to be respectful and sensitive in their communication, it is also important to be clear so the fundamental core of the message does not get cloudy or lost. We owe this to those who work for us. ●

People do not like to find themselves wondering what their leader thinks of them. When they are unsure of the leader's position about them, this produces an atmosphere of insecurity, anxiety, and self-doubt that saps their creative energies. It can also permeate the organizational culture. Therefore, provide people with the assurance that you will always communicate truthfully with them. They will work with a greater level of trust and confidence knowing that they will never have to guess if they are meeting your expectations.

People appreciate when their leaders are honest with them, so in my estimation, there's never a good reason to be deceptive in your communication. I always like to believe that people can handle the truth. In fact, they deserve it!

My mantra to the communities—internal and external—whom I serve is to always communicate "openly, honestly, and in a timely manner." I say it so often that it has become a cliché among those whom I lead, but I keep saying it as a reminder of how effective leaders communicate. Each one of these adverbs makes a significant impact on the way that communication is received by our stakeholders and constituents, and if even one of these descriptors is missing in the way a leader communicates, the communication will be lacking. This is also important for building trust between you and people you serve.

Communicating in this fashion is not just something that I require of others, it is what I require of myself—especially when I communicate with employees. For example, when I became a superintendent, I made sure that my employees would receive weekly updates from me explaining what was happening throughout the school system. I believe that these vital players should be the first line of recipients in a leader's organizational communication strategy. They give their all to the organization every single day; thus, it is necessary for them to stay informed to feel valued. After all, they are a leader's key communicators.

●●● THE PRINCIPLE IN ACTION

A Clear Message for the Entire Organization

As district leaders, we would frequently hold meetings with outside organizations where we would discuss what strategies the school system used to attain its rates of success. In one memorable meeting centered on a grant opportunity we were pursuing, we discussed teacher professional development data. One of the individuals in the meeting noted that while most of the statistics were quite good, the data that stood out the most were around the measure of leadership. Speaking on behalf of the others, he commented how the group agreed that the system's leadership was well organized to lead the change that the grant would potentially fund, but he was puzzled as to how the leadership developed its effectiveness with such a large organization. One of our employees replied, "We think that our leadership scores so high because there has been consistent communication from the leadership from day one. Regardless of who you are in the organization, everyone knows the message!"

For me to hear this comment was huge—an *incredibly* big deal—especially since this came from a teacher. In a school system of our size, it was always tough to communicate with everyone. The fact that our consistent and effective communication was recognized and appreciated was eye opening. It solidified within me what I believe: Leadership extends far beyond the superintendent's office, which means that leadership exists in all classrooms, all schools, and all corners of the organization. It is not about a title.

Lesson Learned

- If you as the leader do not communicate your message to everyone consistently and correctly, you will feel hopeless in every endeavor you attempt. The more communication that occurs, the better likelihood of a consistent message that resonates. ●

Because of the employees' commitment and dedication to the organization, it makes sense that your staff should be the first to know what is going on and what plans the leader is considering for moving the organization forward. Sharing communications with employees before broadcasting them to the community also makes employees feel important. What's more is that it shows you value them. When the communications finally reach the stakeholders and public outside of the organization, it will be these employees who will interface with them and answer any questions. Think about it. A parent will always go to his child's teacher before going to the principal or superintendent.

Most people do not have a problem communicating openly, honestly, and in a timely manner. when there is good news to communicate. It becomes a challenge only when bad things happen because no one likes to be the bearer of bad news. When they are forced to share information about something unfavorable, leaders tend to freeze and don't know what to say in a compelling way. This "communication paralysis" keeps the leaders sitting on the information for a much longer period than is wise, and because of not hearing any information, people begin to buzz about what the organization appears to be "hiding." Thus, people begin to question the integrity of the leaders by saying, "They're not being transparent!" Have we heard that before?

Bad things are going to happen. People know this, and if something bad has occurred, they simply want the leader to address it, not remain silent. After all, since their community has been affected by the crisis, they feel like they deserve some answers—and they're right. People simply want to hear three things from the leader under such circumstances:

1. What happened?
2. Why did it happen?
3. What is the leader going to do to prevent it from happening again?

Further, you can communicate this information succinctly, yet effectively—in one minute:

- It will take ten seconds to discuss what happened.
- It will take ten seconds to discuss why it happened.
- It will take forty seconds to discuss what you will do to ensure that it does not happen again.

Okay, it may not literally be a minute, but you get the idea. When you communicate these three essentials to people during times of crisis, they are generally satisfied. To them, providing such details seems to be quite a simple process. What's so difficult about communicating such facts? When organizations wait too long to deliver news during a crisis, people begin to grow suspicious of their leaders.

Baptism by Fire

On the first day of school during my first year as superintendent, we had a shooting on our largest high school campus; one student shot another student at the school. This was heartbreaking news, but due to prior crisis planning, I understood that precise communication would be vital. After all, we were dealing with the safety of people's most cherished treasures—their children. Since I was out visiting school campuses when I heard about the situation, I headed to the school that was involved. While I was en route, the chief of police had given me a detailed briefing about the incident. Once there, rather than shying away from the conversation, I, along with the chief of police, spoke to members of the press.

While I did not technically call the press conference, it was *my* press conference; if you are the top leader and you are there at the scene, the press conference becomes yours by default, regardless of who called it. Within two days, I had conducted three press conferences to share information with the people who needed it most: our constituents. I communicated the facts: what happened, what we did about it, and what we were going to do to ensure as much as we could that it would not happen again. People were very appreciative of the fact that our county executive, police chief, and I did not hide behind the walls of our offices until things passed over. Instead, we were very forthcoming with our communication, choosing to share the information in an open, honest, and timely manner. This engendered a greater sense of trust among people in the community.

Lesson Learned

- In a crisis, the public wants to hear from its leadership. Therefore, always be prepared to discuss three facts:

(Continued)

When you as a leader try to cover up a scandal or story by not communicating it in an open, honest, and timely manner, the cover-up becomes an even bigger story than the original story itself! While the actual incident may be at the forefront of public conversation for only a few days, a cover-up has much more lasting consequences. Its effects may never go away and could last while the leader occupies his or her position—if not longer. When the trust of the people erodes because of failed communication, it is nearly impossible for a leader to gain it back. The even greater impact is this: no agenda is accomplished.

Over the years, I have heard some leaders comment that they have avoided challenges with open, honest, and timely communication because they feel that communicating in this manner makes them vulnerable and invites criticism of the honest details they have shared about themselves and their administration. When I hear this, my response is simple: You're right. People *will* criticize you, but more than anything, it is your title and your role as a public figure that brings on their criticism. However, you must be secure in both your leadership and your communication style and grow a thick skin to be an effective leader. My grandmother would always tell me this: "If they don't know you personally, don't take it personal." I doubt if that was her original quote, but it has always been useful to me. Think of it this way: It's better for you to be criticized about the way you do

> "You must be secure in both your leadership and your communication style and grow a thick skin to be an effective leader."

things (which, no matter what your actions, is inevitable, so get used to it) than to be criticized as being evasive and dishonest! If you need to choose between these two types of criticism, choose the one that will keep people's trust of you intact. Again, keep in mind that people evaluate you closely based upon how forthcoming you are in your communications. Keep operating in an open, honest, and timely manner, and you can't go wrong.

Communicate Your Story, or Someone Else Will!

As the leader of an organization, it is doubtless that you wear many hats. You are required to be a strategist, motivational speaker, salesperson, politician (remember that you should know politics, but you should not play them), and public relations representative. Public relations professionals recognize that the first person to tell the story gains a significant advantage in shaping the public's perception about the story.

Good, bad, ugly, or indifferent, people want to know what is happening. Now that information travels at the speed of light, people don't want to wait! They want information now! Social media has accelerated this phenomenon. Thus, you have two choices: break the story yourself or allow someone else to tell your story for you. When you break the story yourself, you reap several benefits:

1. You create your own narrative.
2. You can control the level of detail released.
3. You can use the story to not only report information but to report it in such a way that it simultaneously builds the organizational brand and builds your personal reputation as a leader.

When you sit on information and are slow to report it to the public, you open a window of opportunity for others to tell your story for you. This can be problematic for several reasons:

1. The information that others convey might be completely wrong. Most information that is reported from a secondary source is comprised partly of truth and partly of speculation; when you do not give people the information they need, they accept the information they already know or what they believe they know and fill in the gaps with their own assumptions.
2. The secondary source quite possibly will have little to no concern for creating a narrative favorable to you or your organization.
3. Finally, rather than work to develop your organization's brand and your personal reputation, the secondary source might work directly or indirectly to tear down both. Part of the reason for this is that your delay in communicating the information yourself gives the impression that you have something to hide.

Apollo 20 Takes Off

When I was working in Houston as the chief middle school officer, we had a big initiative called Apollo 20. This initiative was our way of attempting to figure out what we could do to transform our district's twenty lowest performing schools. To communicate the *who, what, where, when*, and *why* of Apollo 20, we hosted a press conference, and we created a website for the community to learn more about the program. We recognized that unless we told our own story about Apollo 20, someone else would do it for us. And, believe me, there were quite a lot of people out there who were interested in spreading a story—a different and less favorable one—about Apollo 20.

The outspoken opponents of Apollo 20 attacked the program from the very beginning because they said that the program would cost too much money. Furthermore, they believed that rather than spend money on a program that would benefit a select number of students, the money should benefit all students in the district. These opponents of the program lived in the more affluent areas of the city where the schools were succeeding, not in the areas where the schools were failing, and some did not even enroll their children in our school system. Other challenges to Apollo 20 arose from our having to make tough decisions to rescue the failing schools, and those unpopular decisions focused particularly around personnel, which came with its own level of pushback from the community.

For a program of this magnitude, we had to be strategic and intentional about introducing our story, sharing it frequently and consistently as well as communicating it in various ways. We had to start the story with the why: Why was there a need for such an intensive program? From there, we moved on to what was going to happen,

(Continued)

when it was going to happen, whom it was going to affect, and how everyone could play a part in the change process. Because of this communication strategy, Apollo 20 ultimately took off. This was a true hands-on lesson for me—one I carried on to my next assignment. When I became superintendent in Baltimore County, my staff and I made sure the system school system had its own website that contained a promotional video, a blog, parent testimonials, student testimonials, and other content that supported our change strategy, particularly around our strategic plan. Each day, elected officials, parents, and community citizens frequented the website where they could find a clear organizational message that detailed what we did, why we did it, and what it looked like. Each year, on our stakeholder survey, this was always noted and given high ratings.

Lessons Learned

- A major initiative requires a major message. The message must be well planned and strategic for multiple audiences so everyone understands the why, what, when, where, and how of the initiative.

- Consider a website for major initiatives where updated communication can occur frequently.

- Overcommunicate as much as possible as no one complains about being communicated with too much. It's always the opposite. ●

Throughout my years as a leader, I have developed and nurtured my relationships with the media. There are three key rules by which I operate:

1. Always maintain a positive relationship with the media.

2. Never, *ever* lie to the media.

3. Always know that *everything* you say is on the record.

If you are always straightforward and honest, you will never have to retract anything. Having the media think favorably about you and your organization can be a critical asset, especially since they have the power to create and alter public perception of you and your organization. Rather than resent their power, I recognize it and respect it, especially since I was a former high school newspaper editor. I have also harnessed their power to use it to my advantage and still maintain relationships with people in the media long after I have moved away from an area. They are just that important!

That said, while you can always use the media to tell your story, be cautious that there are always risks involved. Even some of the most seemingly insignificant of details can skew in the wrong direction the public perception of you and your organization. When others tell your story for you, whatever the results—good or bad—they will be your own fault! Without your personal version, every other rendition will be the most important and credible one on the street. Street credibility is essential. Thus, for best results, share your own story so that you can control it—or someone else will do it for you! Believe it.

Organize Your Communication Efforts

If you're a leader, you're probably busier than any other person you know. However, as true as this may be, it does not excuse you from being an effective communicator; you must never be too busy for this essential element to your effectiveness. Remember this: communication cannot be an afterthought or something to discount or disregard because your attention is on other matters. Instead, it plays a key role in your effectiveness and should receive as much time and attention as the other critical matters you manage on a day-to-day basis. Think about it daily because you already do it daily, whether directly or indirectly.

I have found that the best way for busy leaders to ensure that communication efforts remain at the forefront is by preplanning and auto-scheduling them. One recommendation is to create a communication calendar that specifies the messages that you send out on certain days of the year. This type of approach will also help you to maintain relationships despite your own busy schedule. Here are some examples:

- Include all celebration dates that you need to remember, including birthdays and anniversaries of your employees, managers, board members, and key associates.

- Include special messages that you want to send out on special days:

  o On the date marking the start of Thanksgiving break, make a note to send out a message about how thankful you are for their service and how grateful you are to be spending time with your family and friends.

  o On the date marking the start of spring break, schedule a message to go out wishing everyone a fun and safe break.

  o On the various days for boosting employee morale, schedule various days throughout the year when you will send special messages to lift employee morale like Teacher Appreciation Week, Principal Appreciation Month, standardized testing weeks, and so on. Always periodically encourage time with family and friends as this shows you value a work-life balance.

o At the end of the year, encourage your staff with a message that you are rooting for them to finish strong.

Be creative in your organized approach to communicating with those who matter most in your organization. They will never know that you have a calendar where you strategically plan these messages, but they will appreciate your kindness and thoughtfulness when they receive them! I would have countless employees greet me everywhere thanking me for "their" message. With the advancement of technology, it is a lot easier to personalize messages to ensure that every member of your staff feels special.

If your budget will allow, one of the best ways to organize your communication is to hire a communications director or develop a communications team; organizations of all sizes and sectors have them, even if they are outsourced. When making your hiring selection, be sure to choose individuals whose style of communication complements your own. Understand the value of having someone who can operate in harmony with the way you communicate—someone aligned with your vision. You may ask, "What if I am not a communicator?" While all leaders should communicate their messages, the purpose of a communications director is to complement you in areas where you feel unsure. In working together, you two should strategize to deliver a powerful message.

As a communications director needs to be an extrovert, you have to know your comfort level so he or she complements you. For example, I tend to be very open and forthright with people, and I prefer a more personalized style of communication; I answer my own e-mails most of the time, and I enjoy talking personally to employees and to the press. Thus, my communications director had to understand the manner in which I operated. However, a close colleague of mine, who is a superintendent and an extreme introvert, preferred to work behind the scenes and not speak to the press so he hired a communications director who could handle the role of interacting with the press and brief him accordingly when he had to speak with them. Both he and I knew our personal communication style and hired communications directors accordingly.

A communications director or team can help you develop an organized communications plan to guide your verbal or written communication efforts throughout the year and make sure key projects are coordinated and well communicated. They will also serve as the communications arm of your organization, fielding requests, coordinating press conferences, and releasing information to the media. As stated before, my chief communications officer, Mychael, was invaluable in helping to organize and execute my communications strategy and was integral to my effectiveness as a superintendent. Mychael taught me a great deal about communication through his direct and indirect actions. One of the most important lessons that he taught me was this: tell your story up front, and be genuine with it, or else the media will be able to pick right through it.

Individualize Your Communications

We've all done it. For the sake of efficiency, we sent an e-mail to everyone in the organization. In some cases, this is completely acceptable; in other cases, quite the opposite is true. Sometimes, people need to know that you, their leader, know their individual names, that you are aware of their individual accomplishments, and that you care enough to craft a special message just for them. This might seem like a trivial position to take, but every person wants to feel special, important, and recognized by his or her leader. Isn't this why we emphasize personalized learning for our students? They desire to be distinguished as an individual as opposed to a member of a group.

I understand this need, and I respect it. I have always valued everyone who worked with me and for me, and because I still do, I make every effort to recognize and appreciate those individuals for their unique contributions to the organization.

●●● THE PRINCIPLE IN ACTION

Celebrate Big News

In every role, I enjoyed celebrating good news and recognizing schools and their communities when they did well. One year, two of our schools were named National Blue Ribbon Schools—the highest distinction a school can earn. The day I learned of the recognition, I placed particular attention on my communication because such an honor warranted it. I e-mailed a personalized congratulatory message to the teachers and staff at each of the schools, and that evening, I sent a direct voice message to each of the parents of the awarded schools' children.

Because of this effort, both the teachers and the parents recognized that their superintendent was taking his time to acknowledge at a very personal level the accomplishment of the schools, and this meant so much to them. Parents still tell me that winning the award brought them one level of pride, but personalized recognition from the leader of the entire school system made it even more special. In all, it took me no more than two minutes to record the voice message, but that small

(Continued)

amount of effort went a long way. I made it a practice to do this often, and it was widely appreciated by everyone in the district.

Lessons Learned

- Don't miss an opportunity to celebrate exciting news, especially when it involves recognizing individuals on your team.
- As you recognize individuals, make sure you personalize the recognition, when possible.
- People care if the leader recognizes them. ●

Use Every Available Resource to Communicate

Communication for today's leaders is greatly different from communication even as recently as five years ago. Technology has transformed communication by allowing us with the click of a button to disseminate information to large key segments of the population that we serve. I challenge leaders to use *every* available resource to communicate their messages to their key audiences. Let's embrace it! In doing so, you will reach as many people as possible in multiple ways. One thing that you will notice for sure is that people will never complain about overcommunication; they will only complain if they feel that a leader has not corresponded with them. Thus, maximize the technological resources that are at your disposal to broadcast often your communications to the world—or at least the world that you serve.

Social media is one resource that I encourage leaders to maximize for their communication. As a district leader,

I personally used various social media platforms to share my message. As a matter of fact, I had a "verified" Twitter account @DDance_BCPS with over 37,000 followers. These followers included employees, students, parents, elected officials, and other community members who were interested in following my updates. Whenever I wanted to send accolades or celebrate one of my employees as teacher of the year or employee of the month, I publicized his or her name through social media. Any time I visited a school and I saw something extraordinary, I shared the information by tweeting it. If I attended a school event, I tweeted about it. I purposefully used social media to communicate my high level of engagement in our schools and throughout our school system to ensure our community knew I was a connected and involved leader and that I genuinely cared. Then, and even still today, I post about various educational issues like staff development, state standards, teacher evaluation, and federal law to ensure that people understand how a large part of our economy focuses on educating young people. I continue to post numerous leadership topics for the benefit of various types of leaders around the nation. Through all of this, I build relationships and I meet and connect with more people.

We also used the district's social media accounts to communicate breaking news about the schools in the district. For example, if something noteworthy happened in our system, such as the early closing of schools, we sent this information through social media as well. It is a great resource to leverage your message.

I actually caution those leaders who express a reluctance to engage social media platforms for communicating their messages because they are missing a prime opportunity to reach key segments of the population. While time-critical items should be shared utilizing additional avenues, you should also leverage social media platforms. School systems, businesses, and organizations should work with the social media platform to ensure its accounts are authenticated so individuals know the information coming from the account is reliable. Remember: It is your responsibility to share news about your organization first. Social media allows you to do this in the most efficient and cost-effective manner possible. Social media is the way in which the world communicates today. Leaders have to position messages where the world consumes information. Think about this: According to the Pew Research Center, 74 percent of parents use Facebook, which is the most popular social media platform, with an average of 150 friends with 47 percent of them being friends with their children. Social media is definitely a vehicle to communicating effectively. Remember, though, that not all of your community members are social media followers; be sure to also send your message via traditional forms of communication that will ensure all community members have access to the information they need.

●●● THE PRINCIPLE IN ACTION

Sharing the News Too Fast

Leaders who communicate via social media must be cautiously attentive to logistical matters before dispersing messages. This is a lesson that I had to learn the hard way! One morning as superintendent, I was in a meeting, and because of weather conditions, we decided to close schools early. I immediately announced the early closing through my personal Twitter account. Herein was the problem:

While many of the students in the district followed me on my personal Twitter account, many of our teachers did not. Teachers also did not spend time glued to Twitter during the workday. Thus, the students knew about the early dismissal before the teachers, the bus drivers, and anyone else. Needless to say, a panic erupted throughout the system. We had students addressing teachers in classrooms with, "Dr. Dance says we're getting out of school early today! You didn't know?" This faux pas bewildered both teachers and administrators.

This was an *epic* communications failure on my part. I knew that we'd established an early school closing protocol, which included letting the media know, letting the employees know, informing the transportation department, making sure that students received early lunches, and so on. I knew that I had flubbed this one when Mychael came into my office and said, "All right . . . take away his phone!"

Lesson Learned

- Establish a protocol for official communications, and then follow the protocol by letting the system communicate official messages through the system. In this case, after the school system sent an official message, I should have followed up by sending the same notification. Always make sure that there is a solid structure for the way things are to be communicated, and then, don't jump the gun! ●

I recognize that face-to-face communication is ideal; I am old school enough to remember a time when social media did not exist and that if you wanted to socialize with another person, it had to be face to face. I understand that looking in someone's eyes as you communicate with them really is important. I prefer it! However, I also understand that face-to-face contact is not always feasible because of time limits and geographical restrictions. But don't eliminate face-to-face communications from your repertoire. Rely on face-to-face communications for key players who require that level of interaction.

As a district leader, I made sure to communicate with my board members face-to-face because of the critical role that they played. I communicated in the same manner with parents and students. Face-to-face interaction makes people feel significant—important enough that you have taken time out of your hectic schedule to slow down, sit in front of them, look them in the eye, share your message, and patiently listen to their concerns and reactions. This more intimate form of communication helped my stakeholders to be seen, heard, informed, and validated. This is critically important to sustain a needed relationship to get things done.

●●● THE PRINCIPLE IN ACTION

Meet Often for Small Talk

If you are going to be effective as a transformational leader, you will have to find some means of spending time outside the office in an informal situation, such as a meeting for coffee, to convene with key people to build and nurture relationships with them.

For example, three years into my superintendency, I knew that I had to reorganize our school system to elevate it from good to great. However, I also knew that I would have a host of people who would boldly vocalize that the reorganization would cost too much money or was not needed. Not only would they oppose our efforts but they would make sure that they shared their opposition with others. To intercept the opposition, I met for coffee one morning with five individuals who served as our area advisory chairs and thoroughly explained the proposed change and why the change was so important. Afterward,

I fielded their questions. I also followed up individually with them, as needed.

Ensuring that these key players had a comprehensive understanding of the need for the reorganization was critical because theirs were the voices that were going to pitch the idea to their localities. Before I sent them out to represent me and the potential change, however, I knew that it was important to spend some informal time with them over coffee so they could hear my perspective. Due to these relaxed meetings, these individuals understood my goals, went out to represent me in their respective communities, and persuasively explained the needed change. I had ten other similar meetings around that particular initiative before anything became public.

I am intentional about having coffee with people almost every week, but if my week is too hectic to connect with someone in person, I at least reach out with a phone call or a text message to check on them. I also ensure that I schedule time to meet with elected officials to see if there is anything that I can do to assist them and let them know that I am concerned. This is relationship building and advocacy at its best because it allows these important people to realize that I'm interested in offering help rather than just asking for help. Not only does this serve to benefit me by nurturing significant relationships with these key influencers but it also helps me to build political capital with them—and every leader knows that having people with power and influence on your side can be a prime step to winning. If something happens, I know that I can call them, and they will help.

Lessons Learned

- Don't underestimate the value of meeting with individuals for short periods of time for small talk. It will come in handy when big news needs to be shared.

- Relationships build over time. Take the necessary time to build them, as leaders need key influencers sharing important information with their networks occasionally. If the relationship is already built, it makes it a lot easier. •

Because my time is limited, I try to make the best use of it, especially when it comes to communication. As superintendent, I reserved my face-to-face time for individuals who represented stakeholder groups in the school system. For example, I formed a Teacher Advisory Council comprised of twenty teachers from throughout the county who served as some of my eyes and ears on the ground. We met in person periodically so they could help me think through issues and concerns our constituents and stakeholders were facing throughout the county, and then they would go back and report any news to people in their buildings.

I used a similar model for communicating with our students—my clients—with the Student Advisory Council. I also held student town hall meetings twice a year with middle and high school students. At these gatherings, broadcast to students in the district via live stream, the students spoke with me in person, and they had the opportunity to ask whatever they wanted. They got to talk with the "big guy"—as some students would call it—face-to-face, and this was exciting for them. Truth be told, they asked some excellent and tough questions! Once these meetings were over, the students would go back to their respective schools and share their experiences and interactions with their peers. Thus, by making an in-person contact with a representative group of people and sending them back to their fellow students, I was able to have a strong impact on the total populations I served.

View Communication as a Two-Way Street

People oftentimes mistakenly believe that communication is merely a one-way method of addressing an audience.

Communication, however, is much more comprehensive; it is an exchange process. True communication involves speaking, listening, and arriving at a common understanding between two or more parties.

As a leader, you simply cannot afford to do all the talking and then call it communication. It is essential that you view communication as a two-way street—as an exchange of messages,

> "You simply cannot afford to do all the talking. . . . It is essential that you view communication as a two-way street—as an exchange of messages, ideas, and understandings."

ideas, and understandings. When you take this approach to communication, you will find yourself listening more than you are speaking. This is important because you can only learn and grow from others if you are concentrating on them.

●●● THE PRINCIPLE IN ACTION

Community Conversations

As a leader, it is always important to connect with the community you serve by organizing forums where you communicate directly with them. As superintendent, I realized that I served several communities within the school system. To that end, I would hold a twice-yearly breakfast with local community associations. These breakfasts, which lasted about ninety minutes, took place on a weekday morning before everyone went to work. I only spoke for about fifteen minutes to provide any updates about the organization. Then, I just sat back and listened to them. Recognizing that this was their chance to ask

(Continued)

(Continued)

whatever they wanted and receive immediate answers, the attendees asked all kinds of challenging questions on various issues and offered suggestions about how to improve the system. My staff and I documented everything they said, and we thanked them for their valuable feedback.

I used those forums as a means of reconnecting with our community and of keeping a pulse on what they were thinking and feeling. Not only did the members of our community appreciate these opportunities to communicate directly with me but elected officials also liked the meetings. Although they did not address the crowd, they used the gatherings as an opportunity to connect with the community. In turn, their attendance benefited the school system because our total funding came from elected officials. Seeing me interact with the community we served increased the chances that they would fund our programs and initiatives as well as support them. However, having them present also benefited them. If the community was informed and happy, the electorate was happy, and if the electorate was happy, they are more likely to continue voting to keep the elected officials in office. When leaders painstakingly organize their direct communication, everybody wins.

Lessons Learned

- It is essential for a leader to connect and hold conversations with the multiple communities that the organization serves. Schedule the community conversations to ensure maximum community participation. In the previously given case, holding a breakfast meeting was a great way to ensure a good attendance rate.

- In holding conversations, always make sure to balance speaking and to ensure two-way communication. ●

In addition to the Teacher and Student Advisory Councils, I also had a Business Advisory Council. I recognized early on that all organizations are businesses with different missions. My Business Advisory Council was comprised of well-known leaders who advised me about the state of business in the community as well as about pertinent business trends. I met with this special council four to six times per year, and I looked forward to every gathering with them for good reason: instead of doing the talking, at these meetings, I was listening and learning. I absorbed all the expertise they shared about business, and afterward, I strategized with them about how to use the knowledge to improve the operations of our school district. I stayed closely connected to this group of advisers and still have strong relationships with several of the members. Many times, this same group would work with me on a political strategy, advising me on approaches I needed to take when interacting with elected officials.

Communication is a two-way street that involves both talking and listening. It allows you to be constantly learning, growing, and developing, which will ultimately make you a more informed, more effective leader. If you ignore the listening aspect of communication, you limit your own growth as a leader and stand a chance of missing opportunities.

Have an Open-Door Policy

I am always willing to meet and communicate with nearly anybody, and I have always been this way! My open-door policy has made me accessible throughout the years to staff, parents, and students, and in turn, it has made me a more approachable and down-to-earth leader. People like knowing that they can have a meeting with their leader when they have an issue or challenge that needs to be resolved.

When people have a concern, they often want to meet directly with the top leader in the organization because this person has the power to get things done! They want much more than sending an e-mail, leaving a voicemail, or writing a letter. Why not consider meeting with them to show you're approachable?

Let me offer a caveat because I do have a few qualifiers to the open-door policy. In all organizations, but especially in school systems, we must operate according to a sense of protocol to maintain a sense of structure when communicating. For example, if a parent wanted to meet with me about a situation at his or her child's school, there were levels of communication that the parent must have exhausted before being able to meet with me. Only after the parent completed each of these levels would I meet with him or her. If he or she recognized and approached me somewhere out in the community, which happened quite frequently, I would certainly speak with them about their concerns. In fact, there were many times during this informal conversation that I was able to defuse the anxiety. However, I always ended the conversation by advising them to follow the proper lines of communication to have the issue formally resolved. It is all about customer service, and students, their families, and your constituents are our customers.

Another part of my open-door communication policy was encouraging parents and teachers to directly e-mail me. This small step meant the world to my constituents because prior to me, they never had such free access to the system's leader. In previous administrations, the superintendent was virtually untouchable with layers and layers of filters. When I arrived, I completely changed things, and this was a huge victory!

You might be saying to yourself, "You get e-mails from any parent or teacher who wants to send a message? That must take a lot of time out of your day!" You're correct; reading and answering these messages does consume a huge amount of time. But then again, effective leadership takes a time commitment that many are unwilling to acknowledge. I receive hundreds of e-mails a day, and I personally answer every one that appears on my computer screen because there may be a message that could put me in touch with a beneficial contact. Although this daily task is time consuming, it does not interfere with my ability to do my job because my assistant and I developed a system that helped me manage my e-mail. Keep in mind that communication is not something that should divert you from doing your "real" work; it should be a priority that you engage in as strategically and deliberately as you engage in the other things on your daily to-do list.

In some cases, I received e-mails about a need at a certain school, and either my assistant or I worked directly with the community superintendent or the school involved to resolve the matter.

In other cases, when teachers e-mailed me about matters that required more time than I had, my assistant or I would direct other staff members to resolve the issue, and I would follow up to make sure the task was done correctly. Every individual who requested my help knew that I was aware of the concern and that it mattered enough for my team and me to get involved. People do not care that you are personally solving their issue; all they care about is that their issue is solved.

A Simple Thank-You

People at every level of an organization appreciate communication from the leader. Taking the time to be a "reachable" leader can reap significant benefits. For example, as superintendent, I had two e-mail accounts: one address for official business and another address for the personal concerns of my staff. Many superintendents practice this method. One day, I received an e-mail from a bus driver at my official e-mail address. The e-mail simply read, "Can you call me? I have something to share." Ten minutes later, I sent her my cell phone number, spoke with a pleasantly surprised woman, and discovered that her issue was not even about her job; she was just reaching out to thank me for allowing her child to take the SAT exam for free on a special testing day that we had arranged for all students. I could have easily missed the opportunity to hear her express her gratitude if I had not reached out to her. Hearing the joy and appreciation in her voice for simply being able to talk with her leader—something she never thought she'd ever be able to do—reaffirmed for me the importance of being approachable with an open-door policy.

Lesson Learned

- Having an open-door policy does not mean that everyone who comes through it will want something from you. People recognize how hard the leader works and in many instances may just want to say thank you. If the door is closed, it can't be said. ●

This type of communication sends a strong message from the leader who is willing to hear from and help the people throughout an organization. It will help your organizational brand and strengthen your reputation as the leader.

LEADING THROUGH COMMUNICATION NUGGETS

1. Communicate openly, honestly, and in a timely manner, regardless of the message or the audience.

2. Communicate and control your story before anyone else has the opportunity to do it for you.

3. Organize your communication efforts to ensure succinct alignment with the intended message and audience.

4. Individualize your communication to ensure it's personalized appropriately for the audience.

5. Use every available resource to communicate the intended message, including contemporary methods you must acquire to reach the right audience.

6. View communication as a two-way street so you are listening more than you are speaking.

7. Have an open-door policy, which is the best method for communicating with any audience, especially your internal stakeholders—your employees.

Additional Resources

Baldoni, J. (2003). *Great communication secrets of great leaders*. New York, NY: McGraw-Hill Education.

Gilbert, M. B. (2004). *Communicating effectively: Tools for educational leaders*. Lanham, MD: Scarecrow Education.

Harkins, P. J. (1999). *Powerful conversations: How high impact leaders communicate*. New York, NY: McGraw-Hill.

Harvard Business Review. (2011). *Harvard Business Review on communicating effectively*. Boston, MA: Harvard Business Review Press.

Maxwell, J. C. (2010). *Everyone communicates, few connect: What the most effective people do differently*. Nashville, TN: T. Nelson.

Murray, K. (2014). *Communicate to inspire: A guide for leaders*. London, England: Kogan Page.

Patton, B., Stone, D., & Heen, S. (2011). *Difficult conversations: How to discuss what matters most*. London, England: Penguin.

Roebuck, D. B. (2012). *Communication strategies for today's managerial leader*. New York, NY: Business Expert Press.

Sinek, S. (2013). *Start with why: How great leaders inspire everyone to take action*. London, England: Portfolio/Penguin.

CONCLUSION
AVOIDING PITFALLS

A man must be big enough to admit his mistakes, smart enough to profit from them, and strong enough to correct them.

—John C. Maxwell

A commitment to focusing on equity, to understanding and managing change, and to communicating effectively allows us to always give people more than they were expecting. However, as we are striving to become stronger leaders and implementing our vision for our organization, we must be mindful of three leadership landmines that could divert our focus from leading our organizations and could sabotage our future leadership opportunities.

Mistake 1: Knowing All the Answers

My late grandmother always said we have two ears and one mouth because we should listen twice as much as we talked. As it turns out, there was some great truth to this. Some people think they know all the answers. In their minds, they are the smartest people in the room, and as a result, they like to do all the talking. This gives the impression they do not value the thoughts, opinions, and information of others, and this is a grave mistake. To become an effective leader, you need to do more listening than talking. You cannot enter a situation, especially as a new leader, and assume you are completely knowledgeable to address issues or concerns. If you operate in such a way, people will not respect you nor will they passionately devote themselves to the work.

Secondly, when you finally feel you need the opinions of others, you may find that no one is willing to offer any because of your brash attitude. In fact, there is the potential that your employees would just as soon watch you fail. Leaders who talk more than they listen alienate others and develop a brand of being bossy, controlling, and closed-minded. Don't let this be you. Use your ears to listen to anyone willing to talk because something in their words might be vital to your next level of effectiveness.

> "Leaders who talk more than they listen alienate others and develop a brand of being bossy, controlling, and closed-minded."

●●● THE PRINCIPLE IN ACTION

Mr. Know It All

I used to work for someone who felt that he had all the answers. In most cases, the people he was addressing had no idea what he was talking about, but because he was the leader, we all would just sit there and listen, rarely accepting his opinions. He stayed in the position for less than one year. As a leader, understand this: if you are the only one talking, chances are you are the only one who is listening, too! People will ignore you when they realize that the conversation is one-sided and their voices do not appear to matter.

Lesson Learned

- Do less talking and more listening because the opinions of others are vitally important and can help both you and your organization flourish. ●

Mistake 2: Bashing the Previous Leadership
· ·

Invoking my late grandmother again, she always would say, "If you can't say anything nice, do not say anything at all!" This is especially true when you are talking about those who previously served in the role you currently occupy. Think about it: Have you ever wondered why most sitting presidents do not talk about who was formerly in office? There is a good reason!

It is quite common for a new leader to be inundated with complaints from employees and constituents about the many ways in which the previous leader was lacking. As they are communicating their discontent, they will be looking for cues in your face or body language that suggest you understand what they are saying and that you agree with their opinion of the past leader. Since you know nothing about the former leader, don't allow yourself to be ambushed by this situation. Activate your poker face, and politely state that as far as you are concerned, you have nothing to say. Leave it at that!

Do not bash any leader who came before you. Instead, appreciate the fact that the organization has advanced because of the previous leaders' efforts! Be thankful for the good work your predecessors did to lay the foundation for you to take the reins of the organization.

Always be aware that no matter how bad the previous leader might have seemed, in the eyes of some, there will still be people within the organization who are loyal to the individual and appreciate his or her efforts. If you engage in criticizing and attacking the previous leader, loyalists will immediately develop a negative impression of you. By doing so, you could lose points with some key people, ostracizing them from the very beginning because of your lack of respect toward your predecessor.

When you assume the leadership of an organization, take this prudent approach:

1. Recognize the work of the previous administration, honor the past leader(s), and express appreciation for the progress made. (Surely there had to be *some* progress!)

2. Explain that you plan, with everyone's help, to enhance the organization and to advance it to the next level of growth and development.

3. Begin building on the groundwork laid by the previous administration.

This classy, mature approach is sure to gain you favor with everyone in the organization and help to establish you as the new—and soon to be well-respected—leader of the organization.

The Former Principal

I had a colleague who accepted a job as principal of a school that was in rough shape. As opposed to doing some reconnaissance and listening to understand the school's previous status, what created its present situation, and what the team could do to make it better, she chose a different route—a disempowering one. My colleague engaged in bashing her predecessor and voicing this opinion: "If he hadn't done certain things, the school wouldn't be in such bad condition!" Unfortunately, taking such an open position on her predecessor backfired on her. Because the former principal had been so well liked by the rest of the people at the school, he still had their loyalty. Thus, they did not appreciate her berating the former principal, and to show their disgust, they did not listen to anything she said. In the end, she stayed in the position for only about six months.

The positive relationship that should have developed between my colleague and her staff never had the chance to materialize because they felt like they'd been bashed along with their former principal. After all, they were the staff who worked directly by his side, so they were just as much to blame as he was, right? Leaders should always be mindful that when they are defaming the leaders who preceded them, they are also defaming the current staff.

Lesson Learned

- Be very careful about what you say about those who led the organization before you. No bashing! Instead of focusing your conversations on what went wrong with the former leader, focus on talking through what your team can do to progress. Don't look backward as the new leader of an organization. Keep your eyes focused forward. ●

Mistake 3: Speaking Before You Think

Have you ever put your foot in your mouth? We all have at some point. Do you remember how difficult it was to dislodge it? It was harder than you thought, right? I know it was for me, but it was a much-needed lesson to learn. As an educational leader, both as a principal and as a superintendent, I soon recognized that all eyes and ears were on me. People watched and listened *so closely* to *everything* I did and said. I felt like I was under a magnifying glass! They observed my words, my actions, my mannerisms, my companions, and everything else about my life, both public and private. This is all par for the course for a public leader.

Because all eyes—and ears—are on you as a leader, you must be extra careful and responsible about what you are saying and doing. This not only applies to your behavior in the office or on a campus, but it applies wherever you go. Do not think when you go out in public that people will not recognize you because they will. Consequently, as soon as you appear anywhere, all eyes will turn in your direction and remain fixated upon you! Never forget that you are always being watched and listened to, even when it doesn't look like it, so govern yourself accordingly.

> "Never forget that you are always being watched and listened to, even when it doesn't look like it, so govern yourself accordingly."

It's also imperative to keep your integrity in tact by staying consistent in what you say both in and out of the office. For example, do not say that you like working with someone while you are in the office and then once outside of the office express your dislike for that person. People are watching and listening, and though they might not say a word to you about it, you are doing damage to your reputation in their eyes. Someone will observe your inconsistency and talk about it to someone else, and so on, and so on until you have multiple people questioning your integrity. Eventually, your words will get back to the person you were talking about, and these sticky situations are exceedingly hard to reconcile. Remember: it is a very small world. Many times, even if the person accepts your apology, the permanent damage that's been done to the relationship will prevent feelings from ever being the same. Therefore, you should always think before you speak, especially if you dare to speak negatively about someone or something to *anyone*! However, for best results in these uncertain situations, my recommendation would be to refer to the previous advice: if you can't say anything nice, say *nothing*!

●●● THE PRINCIPLE IN ACTION

The Messy Assistant Superintendent

A former direct report to me was promoted to assistant superintendent after five successful years as a school principal. This individual understood instructional leadership, knew how to navigate change successfully, had a wonderful relationship with her colleagues and community, and appeared to understand how to navigate political waters. I saw strong leadership skills in this individual and wanted to support her as much as I could. I firmly believed she would be a perfect fit in her new role.

After her promotion, her humility seemed to go out of the window faster than she was able to move into her new office. Within three

(Continued)

(Continued)

weeks, district and school leaders accosted me to complain about the things she was saying about the school system and how she was the "strongest" assistant superintendent. Bashing her colleagues, the leaders believed this person was not a team player.

While I don't believe in rumors, it is difficult not to address a situation when well-respected individuals approaching the double digits share concerns with you. Although she initially denied the rumors, it was hard to continue the denial when e-mails began to surface validating the rumors. It was tough for her to take her words back. At that point, it was clearly too late. She was demoted after only four months in her position.

Lessons Learned

- Leaders should always keep two things in mind:
  1. All eyes are always on you.
  2. There is always a microphone in front of you.

Therefore, be careful what you say, how you say it, and to whom you say it. One of the worst positions you can put yourself in is to say something without thinking and believe that you can "clean it up" later. Once you've said something, you've said it. You can never take it back.

- Everything you say carries weight. Yours is the voice of authority in people's lives, so whether you say something that you've evaluated seriously or whether you say something on impulse, people will remember what you say when you say it. Thus, commit to being responsible with your words, and think before you speak. ●

The three principles for success outlined in this book require bold leadership, and they are essential to ensure an organization's success. I have benefited from honing these skills through the trials and errors of experience and from emulating excellent leadership role models. I know they are skills that individuals can acquire if they are determined to continuously learn and flourish to serve others better. Our leadership journey defines us, and it plays a huge part in how we approach life.

Every day, we as leaders must continue growing, sometimes by gaining new knowledge through our experiences and at other times by broadening our perspectives about knowledge we have already attained. However, no matter what the complexity of our personal journeys, we must always remain grounded in these three success principles.

It is my hope that as you continue your own leadership journey, you take the time to enjoy it by remembering these last nuggets:

FIVE ADDITIONAL NUGGETS

1. *Keep learning.* No matter what your field of expertise, your job, or your rank, leadership always involves nonstop learning. Read books, attend development and training seminars, keep your skills relevant to the way society is changing and evolving, and stay current with the trends defining the cutting edge of your industry. Every day that you refrain from learning something—anything—is a day that you lose ground as a leader! Commit to learning something new every single day.

2. *Be authentic.* Leadership involves being authentic. Refuse to be anyone but yourself, but always strive daily to be a *better* version of yourself. You are an original. Therefore, why be anyone else? Each of us has habits, tendencies,

(Continued)

(Continued)

and traits we need to reform; however, people deserve
the privilege of meeting you—the *authentic* you—not your
proxy. Each of us is flawed, but we should not try to hide
our frailties. We should allow a person to see us handle
them with the style, grace, and the professionalism of
someone who still feels that they have much to contribute
to the world. As a leader, allow your self-acceptance to
evoke confidence in yourself so you can approach each day
with a genuine commitment to leading.

3. *Maintain your integrity.* Being human means we all will
   make mistakes at times—sometimes more than we may
   want to admit. I know I have made my fair share of them.
   As leaders, when we make mistakes, we need to own them
   to set an example for others who follow us. My mother
   would always tell me for every decision we make, there is
   a consequence. Leaders must know that overreacting to
   standardizing testing, parental concerns, or other issues
   could have a detrimental impact on their career, especially
   when we decide to act unethically or unwisely. It always
   pays to tell the truth. For when we tell the truth, we never
   have to remember what we said. We are not perfect;
   therefore, let us not pretend to be or give the impression
   we are. While there have been times when I have tried to
   be perfect, as I've developed more as a leader, I've realized
   that nothing beats being yourself.

4. *Take calculated risks.* Risk-taking must be calculated and
   not reckless. Leaders must be bold and take risks, when
   appropriate. Kids have only one time in school, and
   we have to make sure we give them the best possible
   experience—the same types of experiences we work so
   hard to ensure for our own children. The stakes are too

high not to think as if there were no box and opportunity to be innovative. Get people to imagine a future they can collaborate to create. Sometimes this will mean challenging the status quo, but remember as I told the *Baltimore Sun* editorial board to make—as John Kotter (2012) put it—"the status quo more dangerous than the unknown."

5. *Enjoy yourself.* Leadership is critical; however, it should also be *fun!* Your role as a leader is one that you should approach with seriousness but not in a state of stress, pressure, worry, anxiety, and even fear.

As you engage in the honest work of leadership, keep things light, upbeat, and cheerful whenever you can. Be intentional about smiling during times when you are feeling the most stress. Handle pressure with poise, handle stress with a smile, and handle critical moments with class so others can look at you and see you are still very much in control of not only your emotions but also the organization! Your team and stakeholders deserve a leader who *enjoys* being at the helm and who administers it with confidence. That person is you!

INDEX

Open-door policy, 99–102
Organization
    acknowledging current state
        of, 39–43, 67
    learning about, 41
    understanding history of,
        36–39, 67
    understanding players in,
        43–57, 67
Organizational culture, 4

People, xx
    appreciation for, 9–13
    change and, 66
    influencers, 44–57
    insider advocate, 54–56
    See also Players
Pew Research Center, 92
Planning, 62
    for communication, 70–71, 86
    See also Strategy, for change
Players, 39, 43–57, 67. *See also*
        People
Politics, 57
Poverty, 13, 21, 22, 29
Powell, Colin, 10
Press conferences, 79, 83
Prioritizing, 64–65

Race, 29
    awareness of, 9
    children's view of, 29–30
    equity equated with, 21
    need to address, 13, 15
    speaking about, 4
Readiness, for change, 57–58
Relationship building, 95
Relationships, 67
    face-to-face communication
        and, 94, 95

with influencers, 48
with media, 84–85
and planning
    communications, 86
Resistance
    to addressing equity, 21
    to change, 51, 57
Respect, 32
Risks, 15, 114–115
Root cause, 27–28, 37
Rumors, 112

Scandals, communication
    about, 77–80
Secondary sources, 82
Small talk, 94–95
Social media, 81, 90–93
S.T.A.T (Students and
    Teachers Accessing
    Tomorrow), 18–19
Strategy
    for change, 42, 43,
        61–67, 68
    leadership as, 56
Student Advisory
    Council, 96
Students
    communication with, 96
    desire for equity, 29–32
Students and Teachers
    Accessing Tomorrow
    (S.T.A.T), 18–19
Students of color, 29.
    See also Race
Support, for employees, 33
Surprises, 73
Suspensions, 8, 9

Teacher Advisory Council, 96
Teamwork, 45–46

Technology, 18
Time commitment, 57
Timing, of change, 51, 53, 68
Transparency, 73
Trust, 39, 41
Truth, 73, 75

"United States of Education,
  The" (Center for Public
  Education), 29
Useem, Michael, 69–70

Values, 7, 9–13

Websites, 84
Welch, Jack, xvii, 69
Work, The, xviii, 26–29

Zero-tolerance
  policies, 8, 9

CΘRWIN
LEADERSHIP

Simon T. Bailey & Marceta F. Reilly
On providing a simple, sustainable framework that will help you move your school from mediocrity to brilliance.

Edie L. Holcomb
Use data to construct an equitable learning environment, develop instruction, and empower effective PL communities.

Debbie Silver & Dedra Stafford
Equip educators to develop resilient and mindful learners primed for academic growth and personal success.

Peter Gamwell & Jane Daly
A fresh perspective on how to nurture creativity, innovation, leadership, and engagement.

Steven Katz, Lisa Ain Dack, & John Malloy
Leverage the oppositional forces of top-down expectations and bottom-up experience to create an intelligent, responsive school.

Lyn Sharratt & Beate Planche
A resource-rich guide that provides a strategic path to achieving sustainable communities of deep learners.

Peter M. DeWitt
Meet stakeholders where they are, motivate them to improve, and model how to do it.

Leadership that Makes an Impact

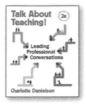

Charlotte Danielson
Harness the power of informal professional conversation and invite teachers to boost achievement.

Liz Wiseman, Lois Allen, & Elise Foster
Use leadership to bring out the best in others—liberating staff to excel and doubling your team's effectiveness.

Eric Sheninger
Use digital resources to create a new school culture, increase engagement, and facilitate real-time PD.

Russell J. Quaglia, Michael J. Corso, & Lisa L. Lande
Listen to your school's voice to see how you can increase engagement, involvement, and academic motivation.

Michael Fullan, Joanne Quinn, & Joanne McEachen
Learn the right drivers to mobilize complex, coherent, whole-system change and transform learning for all students.

CORWIN
LEADERSHIP

A SAGE Publishing Company

Helping educators make the greatest impact

CORWIN HAS ONE MISSION: to enhance education through intentional professional learning.

We build long-term relationships with our authors, educators, clients, and associations who partner with us to develop and continuously improve the best evidence-based practices that establish and support lifelong learning.

Solutions you want. Experts you trust. Results you need.